The Change²¹

Insights into Self-Empowerment

Jim Britt ~ Jim Lutes

With

Co-authors From Around the World

The Change[21]

Jim Britt ~ Jim Lutes

All Rights Reserved

Copyright 2024

The Change

10556 Combie Road, Suite 6205

Auburn, CA 95602

The use of any part of this publication, whether reproduced, stored in any retrieval system or transmitted in any forms or by any means, electronic or otherwise, without the prior written consent of the publisher, is an infringement of copyright law.

Jim Lutes ~ Jim Britt

The Change Volume 21

ISBN# 979-8-8693-9001-1

Authors

Jim Britt

Jim Lutes

Charla Anderson

Natasha Davini, ND

Dr. Allison Snowden

Jerry Roisentul

Crystal Shelton

Annie Mood

Moon Sade

Brian C. Hite

Melissa S. O'Connell

Lisa Burns

Vipin Tyagi

Sgt. Eric C. Weaver (Ret)

Jan Davidson

Tanja Lee

Brian C. Hite, PhD

Sandra Saenz

Lynn Hurlburt

Karen Butler

Cyndy Violette

DEDICATION

To all those who dedicate their life to helping others live a more fulfilled life

PREFACE

By Jim Britt

One of the World's top 20 life and success strategists and top 50 most influential keynote speakers

The only constant in life is change. It swirls around us, weaving through the fabric of our existence, shaping our perspectives, molding our characters, and pushing us toward personal growth. Yet, despite its inevitability, change often comes with a veil of uncertainty and fear. How do we navigate these turbulent waters of transformation? How do we harness its power not only to survive, but to thrive?

"The Change-*Insights into self-empowerment*" is a collective journey into the heart of transformation, a treasury of wisdom from twenty-two diverse voices, each offering a unique perspective on self-empowerment. This anthology is more than a collection of essays; it is a tapestry of experiences, woven together to inspire, guide, and empower readers on their own paths of change.

As the co-creator and publisher of this anthology series, my journey began with a simple question: What does it truly mean to empower oneself in the face of change? The answers unfolded through the secrets and strategies shared by our esteemed coauthors. The depth of their insights reflects the rich tapestry of human experience, and their stories serve as both a mirror and a roadmap for those seeking self-empowerment.

The twenty-two chapters in this book are a testament to the resilience of the human spirit. Each coauthor generously shares their personal journey of transformation, offering glimpses into the moments of struggle, self-discovery and triumph. These writings are as diverse as the coauthors themselves, spanning over thirty countries, cultures, and life experiences. Yet, in their diversity, a common thread emerges—a shared commitment to embracing as a catalyst for personal empowerment.

Within these pages you'll discover several facets of the self-empowerment journey. "Awakening" is where our coauthors explore the pivotal moments that sparked their awareness and sparked their desire for change. Their stories demonstrate the transformative power of self-awareness, the first step on your own path to empowerment.

Next is "Resilience" where you can delve into the challenges our coauthors faced and the strength, they found within to overcome diversity. Whether dealing with loss, facing unexpected detours, or navigating the complexities of personal relationships, or in business, these stories illustrate the transformative nature of resilience and the inherent power within us to adapt and persevere.

Next, you'll find "Empowerment" which is the celebration of the intentional choices made by our coauthors to take charge of their lives. Through conscious decisions, mindset shifts, and a commitment to personal growth, they found the keys to unlocking their true potential. These stories and insights serve as beacons of inspiration for readers seeking to actively shape their own destinies.

And finally, "Integration" as our coauthors reflect on the ongoing journey of self-discovery and personal change. They share their practices, philosophies, and lessons that continue to guide them as they navigate the ever-changing landscape of life. These stories offer a roadmap for readers to integrate and sustain their newfound empowerment into their daily lives.

"The Change" is an invitation to explore the depths of your own potential, to embrace the certainty of change with open arms, and to recognize that within every challenge lies an opportunity for growth. It's a guide for those who seek not to just survive change but to harness its transformative power for a more empowered and fulfilling life overall.

So, as you embark on the journey through the pages of this volume of "The Change" I encourage you to approach each chapter with an open heart and curious mind, realizing that just one good idea acted upon can profoundly change your life. Let the stories and strategies shared by our coauthors be a source of inspiration, guidance, and confirmation that you too possess the power to navigate change with grace and determination and emerge stronger on the other side.

May this anthology serve as beacon of light, illuminating the path of self-empowerment and inspiring you to embrace the infinite possibilities that arise when you courageously and openly welcome change into your life.

With Gratitude and anticipation! Look forward to hearing your success story!

Jim Britt

http://JimBritt.com

FOREWORD

By Les Brown

Many of us spend at least a good part of our day going over internal dialog. We relive past experiences, worry about the future, blame the outside world for our shortcomings and criticize ourselves for not having all we want by this point in our lives. We do this both consciously and unconsciously. Even while we are listening to others, we aren't really fully present. Instead, we are rehearsing our answers, slipping back into yesterday and worrying about tomorrow.

We live in uncertain times. We all feel we have minimum control over being able to change external circumstances, but we do have control over being able to change our internal environment, not only being able to see the truth behind a given situation but also how we respond to it. And to get the best out of the most stressful times, we need to demand the best from ourselves.

Many feel the pain of unhappiness. So many suffer from it daily, unaware that they can eliminate their suffering and find happiness by simply seeing the truth behind their unhappiness and making the right choices to change it. The problem is that our emotional conflicts are so familiar to us that they keep us blinded to better possibilities. We actually become addicted to feeling the way we do, thinking that it is just the way things are and we resign ourselves to getting by and coping.

I have had the privilege of speaking for over forty years serving millions of people from over 51 different countries. I know that there are certain patterns that create success and other patterns that breed internal conflict and failures.

The secret to being fulfilled and living the life you want is having the courage to go beyond the skills you've learned and discover the gifts that you were born with and to implement them daily. So many people settle for less in life, but I can tell you from my experience that it doesn't have to be that way.

I was born in an abandoned building on the floor with my twin brother in a poor section in Miami Florida called Liberty City. When we were six weeks of age, we were adopted by Mrs. Mimi Brown. Whenever I speak, I always say that all that I am and all I ever hope to be I owe to my mother.

When I was in the fifth grade, I was labeled educable mentally retarded and put back from the fifth grade to the fourth grade and failed again when I was in the eighth grade. Mrs. Mimi Brown took my brother and I and five other kids in as foster kids and eventually adopted us.

Because of the work that Jim Britt does and the methods and techniques he uses to change your story and how you see yourself, it enabled me to build my career to make it against all odds. Both Jim Britt and Jim Lutes are icons in personal development and empowering others to be the best they can be.

You have something special inside. You have greatness in you. When you read this book, it will take you on a journey and introduce you to a part of yourself that has remained hidden and you didn't know existed.

When you begin to look at your goals and dreams realize that you have greatness inside you. "The Change" will provide the insights and processes of self-development that will empower you to manifest your greatness.

Jim Britt and I actually started the foundation of our speaking careers in the same direct selling company, Bestline, over 40 years ago. Although I haven't followed Jim Britt's career over the years, I do know that he is recognized as one of the top thought leaders in the world, helping millions of people create prosperous lives, rewarding relationships and spiritual awareness. He has authored 15 books and multiple programs showing people how to understand their hidden abilities to do more, become more and enjoy more in every area of life.

Today, Jim Britt and mind programming expert, Jim Lutes, along with inspiring co-authors from around the world, bring a pioneering work "The Change" book series to the market to transform lives. Their principles are forged on touching millions on every continent.

As you read, you are exploring self-empowerment principles from a whole different perspective. In fact, Jim and Jim's publications of The Change book series now has hundreds of coauthors in 26 countries. The real power in each book is that 20 coauthors share their inspiring story so that the reader may benefit from their experience. It is packed with life-changing ideas, stories, tips, strategies on various empowering topics that you will love.

The principles, concepts and ideas within this book are sometimes simple, but can be profound to a person who is ready for that perfect message at the right time and is willing to take action to change. Maybe for one it's a chapter on relationships or leadership. For the next maybe it's a chapter on forgiveness or health awareness, and for another a simple life-changing message like I received as a youngster from a teacher. Each chapter is like opening a surprise empowering gift.

As I travel the world presenting my seminars, I meet people who spend more time and energy focused on what's wrong with society and their lives than is spent on helping each other improve the quality of life. With so much time spent on social media we often fear intimate contact with each other. Mistrust is often our first reaction. We judge and sometimes brutalize those among us who are in any way different from ourselves. We become addicted to anything that allows us a brief consolidation from the terrible pain we feel inside.

We need to begin to understand more about ourselves and our condition if there is ever to be the possibility of a healthy society. I believe this is possible and that's why I am so passionate about the work I do. Simply put…we are at war with ourselves. Real healing only takes place when we are willing to experience and face the truth within.

The conclusion to me is an exciting one. You, me and every other human being are shaping our brains and bodies by the thoughts we think, the emotions we feel, the intentions we hold, and the actions we take daily. Why is it exciting? Because we are in control of all these things and we can change as long as we have the intention, willingness and commitment to look inside, take charge of our lives and make the changes.

Whether you're pursuing, your dreams as an entrepreneur, a business owner or you want a more fulfilling relationship, or simply want to live a happy life, being authentic and actively appreciating what you're really capable of is going to be one of the most important assets you possess. It will make the difference between just "getting by" and really thriving and experiencing happiness or internal conflict.

Self-knowledge provides you with the emotional edge that will help you create a better life not only for yourself, but also for everyone with whom you come in contact.

This is the time to extract the best out of yourself and to use that gift to touch the lives of others.

I want to congratulate Jim Britt and Jim Lutes for making this publication series available and for allowing me to write the foreword. I honor them both and the coauthors within this book and the series for the lives they are changing.

As you enter these pages, do so slowly and with an open mind. Savor the wisdom you discover here, and then with interest and curiosity discover what rings true for you, and then take action toward the life you want.

Be prepared…because your life is about to change.

Hope to meet you one day at one of my seminars. And remember, everything you do counts!

Les Brown

Table of Contents

PREFACE vii

FOREWORD xi

Jim Britt 1
    Think Like Superman

Jim Lutes 13
    What You do with YOU

Tanja Lee 33
    Courage is The Key to Self-Empowered Change

Brian Blatt 43
    Breaking Through the Invisible Barrier of FEAR

Cyndy Violette 51
    The Life of a Poker Legend

Brian Hite 57
    Begin Again: Mastering the Art of Resilience 58

Crystal Shelton 69
    Transforming Stress into Serenity

Charla Anderson 81
    Unleashing Potential: A Journey of Transformation and Empowerment

Jerry Roisentul 91
    Transforming Failures into Victory: My Journey of Overcoming Doubt and Fear and Cultivating a Resilient Mindset.

Karen Butler 103
    The Magic of KBFIT: Change Your Mind – Change Your Body – Change Your Life.

Lisa Burns **113**
  Beauty From Ashes

Eric C. Weaver **121**
  Overcoming The Darkness: Shining light on Mental Illness, Trauma, and Suicide in Law Enforcement.

Jan Davidson **131**
  Understanding the Behaviors of Grief: Recognizing Grief Beyond the Surface

LS Kirkpatrick **143**
  Phenomenal Me!

Natasha Davini **151**
  Igniting your inner Phoenix.

Sandra Saenz **161**
  Streaming the Supernatural: Your Birthright: "Listening is a talent. Streaming your source is a superpower."

Melissa S. O'Connell **173**
  The Biggest Obstacle We'll Ever Overcome

Annie Mood **183**
  From Adversity to Empowerment – Own Your Power

Lynne Hurlburt **195**
  Don't Stop

Moon Sade **205**
  Embracing Courage: My Journey of Awakening

Vipin Tyagi **215**
  Following Our Inner Whispers

Afterword **224**

Jim Britt

Jim Britt is an award-winning author of 15 best-selling books and nine #1 International best-sellers. Some of his many titles include Rings of Truth, Do This. Get Rich-For Entrepreneurs, Unleashing Your Authentic Power, The Power of Letting Go, Cracking the Rich Code and The Entrepreneur.

He is an internationally recognized business and life strategist who is highly sought after as a keynote speaker, both online and live, for all audiences.

As an entrepreneur Jim has launched 28 successful business ventures. He has served as a success strategist to over 300 corporations worldwide and was recently named as one of the world's top 50 speakers and top 20 success coaches. He was presented with the "Best of the Best" award out of the top 100 contributors of all time to the Direct Selling industry.

For over four decades Jim has presented seminars throughout the world sharing his success strategies and life enhancing realizations with over 5,000 audiences, totaling almost 2,000,000 people from all walks of life.

Early in his speaking career he was Business partners with the late Jim Rohn for eight years, where Tony Robbins worked under Jim's direction for his first few years in the speaking business.

As a performance strategist, Jim leverages his skills and experience as one of the leading experts in peak performance, entrepreneurship and personal empowerment to produce stellar results. He is pleased to work with small business entrepreneurs, and anyone seeking to remove the blocks that stop their success in any area of their life.

One of Jim's latest programs "Cracking the Rich Code" focuses on the subconscious programs influencing one's relationship with money and their financial success.

www.CrackingTheRichCode.com

Think Like Superman

By Jim Britt

"Waking up to your true greatness in life requires letting go of who you imagine yourself to be."

--- Jim Britt

FACT: Becoming a millionaire is easier than it has ever been.

Many people have the notion that it's an impossible task to become a millionaire. Some say, "It's pure luck." Others say, "You have to be born into a rich family." For others, "You'll have to win the Lotto." And for many they say, "Your parents have to help you out a lot." That's the language of the poor.

A single mother with five children says, "I want to believe in what you're saying. However, I'm 45 years old and work long hours at two dead-end jobs. I barely earn enough to get by. What should I do?"

Another man said, "Well, if you work for the government, you cannot expect to become a millionaire. After all, you're on a fixed salary and there's little time for anything else. By the time you get home, you've got to play with the kids, eat dinner, and fall asleep watching TV."

Everyone has a story as to why they could never become a millionaire. But for every story, excuse really, there are other stories OR PEOPLE with worse circumstances, that have become rich.

The truth is that all of us can become as wealthy as we decide to be, and that's a mindset. None of us is excluded from wealth. If you have the desire to receive money, whatever the amount, you have all of the rights to do so like everyone else. There is no limit to how much you can earn for yourself. The only limitations are what you place on yourself.

Money is like the sun. It does not discriminate. It doesn't say, "I will not give light and warmth to this flower, tree, or person because I don't like them." Like the sun, money is abundantly available to all of us who truly believe that it is for us. No one is excluded.

There are, however, some major differences between rich and poor people. Here are some tips for becoming rich.

Change Your Thinking

You have to see the bigger picture. There are opportunities everywhere! The problem is that most people see just trees, when they should be looking at the entire forest. By doing so you will see that there are opportunities everywhere. The possibilities are endless.

You'll also have to go through plenty of self-discovery before you earn your first million. Knowing the truth about yourself isn't always the easiest task. Sometimes, you'll find that you are your biggest enemy—at least some days.

Learn from Millionaires

Most people are surrounded by what I like to call their "default friends." These friends are acquaintances that we see at the gym, school, work, local happy hour, and other places. We naturally befriend these people because we are all in the same boat financially. However, in most cases, these people aren't millionaires and cannot help you become one either. In fact, if you tell them you are going to become a millionaire, some may even tell you that it's impossible and discourage you from even trying. They'll tell you that you're living in a fantasy world and why you'll never be able to make it happen. Instead, learn from millionaires. Let go of these relationships that pull you down when it comes to your money desires. It's okay to have friends that aren't millionaires. However, only take input from those that have accomplished what you want to accomplish. Hang out with those that will encourage and help you get to the next level. Don't give your raw diamonds to a brick layer to be cut.

Indulge in Wealth

To become wealthy, you must learn about wealth. This means that you'll have to put yourself in situations that you've never been in before.

ON OCCASION, DO SOME OF THESE:

Fly first class and see how it makes you feel.

Eat out at the finest restaurant and don't look at the price.

Take a limo instead of a cab or Uber. Watch how you feel.

Reserve a suite in a first-class hotel.

If you are used to drinking a $20 bottle of wine, go for the $100 and see how it tastes. It does taste different.

All I am saying is, try some of the things that wealthy people do and see how it makes you feel.

Believe it is Possible

If you believe that it is possible to become a millionaire, you can make it happen. However, if you've excluded yourself from this possibility and think and believe that it's for other people, you'll never become a millionaire.

Also, be sure to bless rich people when you can. Haters of money aren't likely to receive any of it either.

Read books that have been written by millionaires. By gaining a well-rounded education about earning large sums of money and staying inspired, you'll be able to learn the wealth secrets of the rich. I just saw a video on LinkedIn with my friend Kevin Harrington from the TV show Shark Tank. He said that one of his new companies just had a million-dollar day on Amazon.

Enlarge Your Service

Your material wealth is the sum of your total contribution to society. Your daily mantra should be, *'How do I deliver more value to more people in less time?'* Then, you'll know that you can always increase your quality and quantity of service. Enlarging your service is also about going the extra mile. When it comes to helping others, you must give it everything you have. You just plant the seeds and nature will take care of the rest.

Seize ALL Opportunities That Make Sense

You cannot say "No" to opportunities and expect to become a millionaire. You must seize every opportunity that has your name on it. It may just be an opportunity to connect with an influential person for no reason. Sometimes the monetary reward will not come immediately, but if you keep planting seeds, eventually you'll grow a fruitful crop. Money is the harvest of the service you provide and sometimes the connections you have. The more seeds you plant, the greater the harvest.

Have an Unstoppable Mindset

Want to know some of what my first mentor shared with me that took me from a broke factory worker, high school dropout, to millionaire?

First, he said, you have to start thinking like a wealthy, unstoppable person. You have to have a wealth mindset. He said that wealthy people think differently. He said, "I want you to start thinking like Superman!" Sounds crazy, right? Well, it's not. It's powerful and here's why. How you think will change your life.

Wealthy people think differently. They really do. And anyone can learn to think like the wealthy.

I'm not talking about positive thinking, Law of Attraction, or motivation. Let's get real. None of that stuff works anyway. Otherwise, we would all be rich and happy already. I'm talking about thinking based on quantum physics science. Once you understand and apply it, it will change your life. You will become unstoppable!

If there was any person, fictional or real, whose qualities you could instantly possess, who would that person be? Think about it. Personally, I would say that Superman is the perfect person. Now, you are probably thinking I have lost it, right? Just stick with me here. I think you will like what you are about to hear.

Superman is a fictional superhero widely considered to be one of the most famous and popular action hero and an American cultural icon. I remember watching Superman every Saturday morning when I was a kid. I couldn't get enough. He was my hero!

Let's look at Superman's traits:

Superman is indestructible.

He is a man of steel.

He can stop a locomotive in its tracks.

Bullets bounce off him.

He is faster than a speeding bullet.

No one can bring him down.

He can leap tall buildings in a single bound. Great powers to have in this day-and-age, wouldn't you say? What else would you need?

Now, for all you females, don't worry, we have not left you out. There is also a female version of Superman, named Superwoman. She has the same powers as Superman.

Now, this is where it gets interesting. Let's first look at the qualities that Superman possesses that you want to make your own. And to make it simple, I will refer to Superman for the rest of this message, and you can replace with Superwoman if you are female.

Again:

Superman is powerful and fearless.

Superman is virtually indestructible—except for kryptonite of course.

Superman can stop bullets.

Superman has supernatural powers. He can see through walls.

Superman can stop a speeding locomotive.

Superman can stop a bullet.

Superman jumps into immediate action when troubles arise.

Superman can crash through barriers.

Superman can even change clothes in a phone booth in seconds. Not too many of those around anymore. You'll have to duck behind a building to change.

So, you're thinking right now, *'Ok, I know that Superman has incredible supernatural powers, how can that help me? What good will it do me to think I am Superman, a fictional character?'*

Here is where science comes in. This is the part where you will be amazed when you learn about the supernatural powers that you already possess! NO, REALLY!

Your brain makes certain chemicals called neuro peptides. These are literally the molecules of emotion, like love, fear, joy, passion, and so on. These molecules of emotion are not only contained in your brain they actually circulate throughout your cellular structure. They send out a signal, a frequency much like a radio station sending out a signal. For example, you tune to 92.5 and you get jazz. Tune to 99.6 and you get rock. And if you are just one decimal off, you get static. The difference is that your signal goes both ways. You are a sender and a receiver.

You put out a signal, a mindset, of confidence about your financial success and people, circumstances, and opportunities show up to support your success. When you put out a signal of doubt and uncertainty and you receive support for your doubt and uncertainty. You've been around someone that you didn't trust, or you felt less than positive just being in their presence, right? You have also been around people that inspire you. That's what I'm talking about. You are projecting a frequency, looking to resonate with the frequency you are transmitting.

Anyway, the amazing part about these cells of emotion is that they are intelligent. They are thinking cells. These cells are constantly eavesdropping on the conversation that you are having with yourself. That's right. They are listening to you! And others are listening to your cells as well. Others feel what you feel when they are around you.

Your unconscious mind, your cells, are listening in, waiting to adjust your behavior based on what they hear from you, their master. So just imagine what would happen if you started to think like Superman...or like a millionaire.

Here are some of the thoughts you might have during the day:

"The challenges I face day today are easily overcome, after all I am Superman."

"I am indestructible."

"I have incredible strength."

"Nothing can stop me.....NOTHING."

"I have supernatural powers and can overcome anything."

"I can accomplish anything I want when I put my mind to it."

"I can break through any barrier."

"I can and I will do whatever it takes to accomplish my goal."

"I fear nothing."

The trillions of thinking cells in your body and brain listen, and they create exactly what you tell them to create. Their mission is to complete the picture of the you they see and hear when you talk to them. They must obey. It's their job!

Since you are Superman, you cannot fail. Why? Your thinking cells are now sending out the right signal, because you told them to. They are making you stronger, more successful, every day! You have the ability to fight off all negativity, doubt, fear, and worry—nothing can stop you!

Superman has total confidence. So, your cells of emotion relating to confidence will now create more neuro peptide chemicals to promote feelings of power and confidence that others will feel in your presence.

Superman is fearless. So, your cells of emotion relating to fear will now create more neuro peptide chemicals to create feelings of courage. You are unstoppable!

And here's the key. Others will respond to you in the same way that you are talking to yourself.

If you are confident, others will have confidence in you.

You have thousands of thoughts every day. Make sure your thoughts are leading you in the direction you want to go. Make sure you are telling your cells a success story, and not a 'woe is me' story.

Most have been conditioned to think that creating wealth is difficult, or that it's only for the lucky few. What do you believe? It doesn't cost you any more to think like Superman; and it's much more inspiring!

Mediocrity cannot be an option if you decide to be wealthy and think like Superman.

Your decision, and communication with your cells, creates a mindset; that mindset influences how you show up.

None of that old type of thinking matters anymore...after all, you are Superman, and you can accomplish anything.

If you want wealth, you have to stretch yourself. You have to do the things that unsuccessful people are not willing to do. You have to say "yes" to opportunity, then figure out how to get the job done.

Maybe you are uncomfortable selling and asking for money. If that's the case, then learn sales and learn to ask for money every day until you feel comfortable asking for it. You will never have money if you don't learn to ask for it.

I've learned a lot in the past 40+ years as an entrepreneur. I've learned that in order to have more, you have to become more. I've also learned that if you are comfortable, you are not growing. I learned that I couldn't go from a nervous rookie speaker with minimal self-confidence to hosting TV shows and speaking in front of 5,000 people overnight. I simply wasn't ready. I grew into that, one speaking engagement at a time. Every time I finished a speaking engagement, I would ask myself, "How did I do, and how could I do it better?" I still do that today.

And I've learned from the hundreds of thousands of people I've trained, coached, and mentored that none of us can do something we don't believe is possible. It's not going to happen if you're not ready to step out of your comfort zone and stretch yourself.

This has led me to understand the single most important principle of wealth-building, that has meant the difference between poverty and riches for people since humans first traded for pelts.

Are you ready?

Come in just a little closer. Listen up!

Every income level requires a different you, a different mindset! If you think that $10,000 a month is a lot of money, then $100,000 a month will be completely out of reach. If you believe that having $5,000 in the bank would make you rich, then $50,000 won't miraculously appear. You will never earn more money than you believe is "a lot" of money.

What you do as a business is only a small part of becoming rich. In fact, there are thousands, if not tens of thousands, of ways to make money—and lots of it. What I've learned over the years is that, by focusing on who you want to become instead of what you need to do, you're going to multiply your chances of getting rich a hundred-fold.

Ask anyone who's found a way to make a large sum of money legally, and he or she will tell you that it's not hard once you crack the code. And cracking the code starts with you and your mindset. The "code" to which I refer isn't a secret rite or ancient scroll. It's not even a secret. It's a certain way of thinking and believing in which you've trained your mind to see money-making ideas.

That's where you see a need in the marketplace, and you jump on the idea quickly. It might involve creating a new product; or, it may just be teaching others a special technique you've learned. It may even require raising capital to start a company or to market a product or idea on social media.

Don't Hold Back. You Have to Take Action to Change.

Start right now to imagine yourself as already having wealth. How would your life be? How would your day unfold? Start to own your wealth mindset now! The subconscious mind is unable to differentiate between actual fact and mere visualization. So, by imagining that you already have it, you're encouraging your subconscious mind to seek the ways and means to transform your imaginary feelings into the real thing.

Find yourself some mentors. Nobody has all the answers. Surround yourself with people that will support, inspire, and provide you with answers that keep you moving in the right direction. If you truly want to attain wealth, have a thriving business, or reach the top of your game in any endeavor, having a qualified mentor is essential.

Okay, lets come in for a landing ...

It is absolutely essential to have a crystal-clear picture of what you want to accomplish before you begin. If you want to attain wealth, you must learn to operate without fear and with a sharply defined mental image of the outcome you want to attain. This comes from thinking like a wealthy person, (like Superman) making decisions like a wealthy person and being fearless (like Superman) when it comes to stepping out of your comfort zone. Look at the end result as something you're already prepared to do, you just haven't done it yet.

Think about this. Your success is something that you have been preventing; it's not something you have to struggle to make happen. The key is to not let fear, doubt, other people, or mind chatter push your success away. You'll find that the solutions taking you toward your goals will come to you in the most unexpected and sudden ways. You don't need the *perfect* plan first. What you need is a perfectly clear decision about your success, the right mindset, the right mentoring, and the ideal way to get you there will materialize.

The greatest transfer of wealth in the history of the human race is happening right now. Are you positioned to get your share?

Remember, in order to get a different result, you must do something different. In order to do something different you must know something different to do. And in order to know something different, you have to first suspect that your present methods need improving.

THEN, YOU HAVE TO BE WILLING TO DO SOMETHING ABOUT IT.

***

For more information on Jim's work:

www.JimBritt.com

www.PowerOfLettingGo.com

www.CrackingTheRichCode.com

www.facebook.com/jimbrittonline

www.linkedin.com/in/jim-britt

To find out how to crack the rich code and change your subconscious programming regarding your relationship with money: www.CrackingTheRichCode.com

Jim Lutes

Say the name Jim Lutes and chances are a top performer in your company has attended one or more of his dynamic trainings over the last few years.

Having taught his branded form of human performance since the early 1990s, Mr. Lutes has accelerated top level entrepreneurs throughout his career by conducting training on personal growth and subconscious programming into worldwide markets.

During this time Jim took his skills regarding the human mind, and combining it with training on influence, persuasion and communication strategies he launched Lutes International in the early 1990s. Based in San Diego California Jim has taught seminars for, corporations, sales forces, individuals and athletes. Having appeared on television, radio and worldwide stages, Jim's style, knowledge and effectiveness provide profound results.

"Jim Lutes possesses a unique ability to create performance change in an individual in a fraction of the time it takes his competitors". The core of human decisions is based on the programs we acquire, reinforce and grow. Combining Jims various trainings individuals can reach new levels of achievement and fulfillment in all areas of life. The results are at times nothing short of astonishing.

"My goal is to take that embryonic greatness that exists inside every person in America, foster it, empower it and then hand them personal strategies based on solid principles that allow them to take that new attitude and apply it to creating a life masterpiece".

What You do with YOU

By Jim Lutes

Most people think that if they can just learn enough, earn enough, get smart enough, then they will BE enough. And they think that when that happens, they can finally relax and be happy. But what happens is that they get so caught up in what they are constantly *doing* that are not focused on how they are *being*.

In other words, they are not focused on their emotional state. When you engage your emotions your subconscious mind begins to get the messages and begins to establish new rules and new behaviors. Then, it becomes a way of life and enters your heart and really begins to come from your heart. When it is in your heart then it is truly part of you. When you are really getting it at the deepest level, is when you can begin to anticipate what I am going to say, you know you understand it at a much deeper level right now.

I began to study human performance as a way to make some changes in my own life and when I began to see some serious results, I got so excited about it that I wanted to share it with other people. So I committed my life to learning and sharing what works with others. So, I am a committed lifetime learner and therefore I have been fortunate enough to have had the ability to look at and study just about every approach there is to personal development and success that is available in today's market. I am a strong advocate of clear, simple, workable approaches that get dependable and lasting results.

Because of the vast wealth of information my Life Masterpiece teaching gives you and the amazing results you will get, you will likely find yourself returning to it again and again throughout your life.

No matter how successful we are, or how successful we become, we all need a coach to encourage us, to challenge us, to remind us to live up to our potential. I am going to be here to do that for you each day, and it is both my honor and my privilege to serve you in that way.

Let's get started now.

The person that you are, and that person that you must become in order to put the colors of your life masterpiece where you want them and blend them in just the right combination to create your own unique experience might right now seem like two very different people, but they are one in the same. You are that person right now. I am going to help you uncover your true identity and purpose so that you can then activate the universal laws and make them work for you.

When we let go of all the stories, we have been telling ourselves about who we think we are supposed to be and what we think we are supposed to do and have, we not only free ourselves we free our families, our children, our intimate partners, and our friends in the process. There is no way you can make a difference in yourself without touching somebody else even if it is not your intention.

The Life Masterpiece focus is about what you can do with YOU. If you want to change any circumstance, any relationship, then you must begin with yourself no matter how convinced you are that somebody else or something else must change. Changing yourself can change even the most rigid system and stubborn person. And ANY progress moves you forward. And any movement forward on your part creates the opportunity for every other part of your life to be moved forward as well.

One of the most effective ways for you to reprogram your mind is through what I like to call vicarious experiences. These are the experiences other people have had and I will bring you through their experiences by sharing their stories with you. These stories are not in this book simply to fill it up and make it fat like you find in some books. These stories are the heart and soul of the book because this is how you will begin to reprogram your subconscious and take the information into your heart where it will transform you.

The reason why vicarious experiences are so powerful is because they relate to you and so when you are reading these stories your conscious mind will get go and your unconscious mind will get the lesson.

And when you read some of these remarkable stories and meet some of these people who have gone through some amazing personal transformations, you will begin to realize that no matter who you are, no matter what part of the world you are from or what culture you grew up in, whether you grow up poor, wealthy or somewhere in between, whether you grow up with religion or Monday Night Football, you will begin to realize that we all have the same problems.

So what will happen is you will begin to connect with these people because they have the same problems you have- the same challenges. They are universal. You will then see what the reason for this is that we all have the same basic needs, our lives are about meeting these needs and that they impact and determine every single thing we do and every decision we make.

Every single habit, behavior, rule or pattern is your unconscious way of trying to get your needs met. And your needs are the same exact needs every other human being on the planet has. We all use different behaviors to get these needs met but they are still the same.

Some of the behaviors we use are positive and healthy and some of them are not quite so resourceful. And this is one of the reasons why even though we all have the same needs and the same problems, we all get different results. We are hard wired with the same needs, but not with the same subconscious programming. And the reason why we all get different results boils down to one thing- standards.

You know, so often in life, we find ourselves in a position where we live life a certain way. We act a certain way. We were raised in a certain way. And through our lives in an effort to avoid pain and still meet our needs, we made critical decisions about who we are and how we think we need to be. And so we believe we know who we are.

But the way we have behaved for years is simply an *adaptation*. Something that happened in response to the desire we had to meet our basic needs- to get the love, or respect, or acceptance from a parent, lover, loved one or peers- caused us to make a key decision and adapt to the circumstances around us. We do not ever realize that for years we have been living something that we are really good at but which is not necessarily our true nature.

One of the things you will learn here is that a single decision has the power to change everything in a heartbeat. In fact, when you stay with me through this you are going to learn about a decision, I made perhaps some time ago that determines the choices you have made in the course of your life up until now. Today he made a decision to pick up this book and begin this journey with me and if you will indulge me for just a few hours the decision to pick up this book might be the decision that changes everything in your life from today on.

Now that you've made the decision to read it, I will tell you what this book can really do for you. It will get you to uncover and maybe for the first time really identify how the role models of your life have affected your subconscious decision-making in ways you never dreamed possible.

Without getting into the actual science behind it, a child's brain works much differently than an adult's brain. As you might already know our brains operate using four different wavelengths -- alpha, beta, theta and delta. Most of the time, the adult brain operates at the beta level when we are awake. The beta level is when our eyes are focused in our conscious mind is in control, and we are logical. The alpha level is a level that we must pass through to go to sleep and to wake up, and it's also the most common level is one we are in a trance. Theta is for a deeper trance or dreaming, and delta is for deep sleep.

This means that when we are at the alpha level, we are highly impressionable, because the messages are going directly into our subconscious minds. A child's mind is different because it operates primarily at the alpha level, which is why children are so impressionable. This also means that our parents and other significant people in our childhood had a tremendous impact on the messages that are subconscious mind received and events from our childhood had a strong impact on our self-image, our identity and how we develop as adults. This is why when we speak about reprogramming the subconscious mind is very important to talk about her childhood and her relationship with her parents. This is not done to point fingers or place blame, but to help us understand some of the reasons for the choices that we make for the patterns that we keep repeating and how they carry over from generation to generation.

Even if you feel like you held your own when you were growing up, and that the relationships that you had as a child -- especially the relationship she had with your mother and father -- were strong, and you feel like you are strong as a result. There are still patterns that your subconscious mind is running that no longer serve you. Because it's the tension, the experience of having to deal with all of the events of your past and even the events that happened before you were born in your parent's past -- all of these experiences affect your decision making, your relationships, your finances, your choices, behaviors and life circumstances, even today.

Even if your childhood was perfect and you feel like you honor, respect and love your parents and adore all of your siblings and even if your parents or your greatest role models, you are still affected on many levels and in many ways. And because you decided to read this book, I believe you have some things you would like to change. If you change anything, first you must learn to reprogram your subconscious mind and part of doing so is to understand that the key decisions you made in the past still impact you today.

Our childhood role models deeply affect both our conscious and subconscious decision-making and behavior patterns. We are all examples, and some of us are warnings. We all, at one time or another, impact other people. This is one of the reasons why I stress that it is so important to live consciously and be an example.

When I ask people about their belief systems and the habits and patterns that basically control their lives, I am often struck by how few of these beliefs and habits were ever chosen by that person on a conscious level. In other words, the rules that are guiding your life about how to BE in your own life very often picked up unconsciously.

It is incredible how common it is that people start this process, and when they begin to reassess their lives and their relationships with themselves and others in the success they are having or perhaps not having, they discover that much of what has been screwing up their lives, their achievements, their finances, their careers, their intimate relationships, and even their bodies (and I am not talking about the excuse many of us use about genetics. Being the reason, our bodies look the way they do) was influenced by their PARENTS. Not by their parents' problems necessarily, but by somehow trying to be liked, loved or appreciated by one parent. Many times, these decisions also have to do with trying to avoid pain that was inflicted by a parent or other significant role model, or simply standing up to a parent.

We can be 40, 50 or even 80 years old, and we are still living the strategies of a child.

And what's even worse, is it very often when we were a kid, we said, "I'll never be like that!" And here you are today, exactly like that! You don't want to admit it but if you held up a mirror and watched a film of your interactions you would say, "Oh my God, I never wanted to be like that parent." And yet you are. Or perhaps you have done the opposite. Perhaps you have thrown the pendulum the other way and you're not like that parent at all. Now, you are something worse. Or, let's just say you are something else. You are the opposite of the extreme you didn't like. And so now you are another extreme, that doesn't work either. Because no one teaches us this stuff, and so it becomes unconscious. We don't even see it. It's part of the invisible fabric of our thinking and our decision-making every single day.

This book will give you a unique opportunity to look deep inside yourself. It will allow you to look inside of your relationships, your decisions about money, and your decisions about your career, your relationship with God or your higher power, and even your body. It will allow you to understand how your own up bringing us may be influenced you and you probably know a lot of the ways it has influenced you, but maybe you'll spot some of the decisions you have made, maybe even one core decision that has affected your identity.

So, what the heck does identity mean anyway? It can be such a big and often loaded word. Well, I believe identity is the strongest force in the human personality. If you want to know what shapes you the most it's not your capability. It's your identity and the rules you have for who you think you are.

And you know what the challenge is? Most of us defined ourselves a long time ago. And when we step outside that definition, we get uncomfortable, because the strongest force in the human personality is the need to remain consistent with how we define ourselves. Later, we will talk about the human needs referred to earlier. One of them is certainty. What this means is that if certainty is one of the deepest needs we have, then if you don't know who you are, you do not know how to act.

Very early in life, we begin to define who we are. We use labels such as loner, aggressive conservative, sexy, successful, loser, rich or poor.

I work for others. I am ugly. I am smart. I am a procrastinator. I am clumsy. I am athletic. I am thin. I am big boned. What happens is these definitions become self-fulfilling prophecies because nobody wants to be disappointed. Nobody wants to live in a place of uncertainty. So, there may be arranging your identity or in your definition of yourself, but it may not be absolute.

The metaphor that you so often hear what we talk about our comfort zone, is that our comfort zone is like a thermostat. We all have our comfort zone, and it is set by our subconscious mind. So, if your subconscious mind has set your thermostat in a particular area of your life, for example how much money you make, that let's say 45°, and if the temperature drops down to 40°, guess what happens? It doesn't meet your identity. In other words, things are not good enough, whether it be mentally and emotionally financially with your weight (which by the way is the primary reason people whose weight tend to gain it back because they lose it before reprogramming their subconscious mind to reset the thermostat) or whatever.

For example, if you drop down to 40° and your finances and 45° is your identity. This means that 45° is what you must have. Or, if you drop down to 70° in your intimacy and 80° is your identity, then this is what you must have. Whatever it is, when you drop below your comfort zone, you will be compelled to drive to make it better automatically. If your body gets out of control, there is a point at which you go, "that's enough!" You are willing to be a little off your identity but not that much. And suddenly you go on the diet suddenly make the change because you feel the pressure that comes with being inconsistent with your own definition of how you think you should be.

But what most of us fail to recognize is that this happens on the other side as well. Your subconscious mind since your mental thermostat at say 45° for your finances or 80° mentally for how close you want to be with your intimate partner, or 70° for how your body should look and feel,

This is not your *goal*. Your goal is something much larger. This is your subconscious comfort zone or your subconscious definition of yourself. For example, you might think of yourself as big boned, but if it suddenly isn't good enough and you really become overweight, then you change to fit your self-image or your definition of yourself in order to get back into that comfort zone. But also, if it gets better than you expected, perhaps, you lose a lot of weight and get really good shape, or perhaps you lead your company in sales for two quarters in a row when you normally come in third or fourth, or perhaps you jump from 70° in your intimacy, and now you have a relationship that is at 90 or even 100°. You have a really hot, passionate relationship with more passion than you ever have before, or you lose three dress sizes instead of one, or you double your income, whatever it is, your subconscious mind starts talking some sense into you. And your brain goes, "Hello, dude what the heck are you doing? You are 70 degree-er, what in heck are you doing way appear at 90? You can't keep that. That's not gonna last. Get back down to 70° before you get hurt or fail or screw it up. You're in over your head. You're not an entrepreneur. You work for other people."

Wherever your subconscious mind has set your comfort zone based on the way you define yourself, you're going to keep adjusting to stay in that comfort zone. So many times, in these types of programs, people challenge you to get out of your comfort zone, which you can't do consciously. You have to go into your subconscious and reset your comfort zone, just like you would the thermostat. And this will keep happening until you reprogram your subconscious mind with a new identity, and the new comfort zone. Before you set out to make any kind of lasting change, you must reset your subconscious comfort zone.

And what do we do when we exceed our comfort zone? Well, what happened is that the drive to make things better stops. And so you stop growing and gradually you drift back until you reach your comfort zone. Or worse, you start to sabotage. The mental air conditioners kick on and bring yourself right back down to where you think you deserve to be based on your subconscious identity.

For example, if the only kind of love you view as a child was abuse, the only kind of life. You knew was living paycheck to paycheck or in debt, or the only kind of lifestyle you ever experienced with sedentary, whatever it is, even though it might be painful. It is what you know. This becomes your comfort zone and therefore provides the certainty that you need. It becomes your self-definition and what you think you deserve. You begin to think -- not consciously, but unconsciously -- this IS love, this is just the body. You inherited, or that wealth is for other kinds of people, or you're not the right kind of person to make certain kinds of social contacts. Of course, this is not your conscious thinking that this is what is going on in your subconscious.

And therein lies the trouble, or perhaps a better way to say it, the shortcomings with many of the programs you may have tried in the past. They pump you up and felt good about it. They motivated you with affirmations and taught you to use visualization. They've even taught you that the universal laws work for everyone. You may have even made some changes, but they did not last. Because when you're taught these things, you know the stuff in your head on a conscious level. But your identity and self-definition is the thermostat of subconscious mind, so before you can make any substantive or lasting change, first you must reprogram your subconscious mind and change who you are at the deepest level. (Green papers).

In other words, you must become the kind of person who has whatever it is that you want. Visualizing it, affirming it, and even living your life by a new set of standards is not going to work long term until this stuff goes from your conscious to your unconscious and finally into your heart. Not only do you have to DO it, and not only do you have to LIVE it, but you also have to BECOME it. And then you will manifest it.

And that is the difference between the stick figure you are drawing now or the paint by numbers life you have been taught to lead and the masterpiece you are now creating. So, for the colors in our masterpiece is to really live consciously, to be an example, then we have to get conscious about what is shaping us and the thing that shapes you most identity.

Someone who is outrageous will behave, say things differently and move differently than someone who believes they are extremely conservative. They will use a different voice, a different way of moving and a different language. Here is my question for you:

When did you come up with this definition?

When did you decide who you are?

When was the last time you updated it?

Maybe it's time to take another look at who you are today. And maybe you don't have to actually give up your identity. Maybe the identity created for yourself is magnificent, but maybe it's time to expand it. Maybe it's time to add to it. Maybe it's time to open up to a new level of freedom and options.

And when you do that there will be a processional effect in all areas of your life, because we are all connected in a cybernetic loop. If I want to change you, I can try to control you, but that will not change anything. Or I can try to change the system, but that will not last or will be futile. Or I can change me into an ID so that everything changes.

For example, if I change the way I treat you, the way I respond to you, my voice my body my feelings and my emotions by respect for you. It will affect the way you feel and the way you respond back. And the same is true with the universe and higher intelligence. Once you change yourself, reprogram your subconscious, become the person you need to become that the things that you want in your life, then you will begin to receive a different response from the universe in a different result in your life. Then begin to experience your life as a masterpiece.

You will learn that what we value controls what we are willing to do or not do -- in our businesses, and our relationships, with our bodies and with our children. Some people get locked in place into a mindset. I call it being committed to your commitment. For example, have you ever been in an argument, and you were so angry that as the argument progressed, you forgot what you were angry about, and it just became about winning? We've all been there and what happens is we get committed to being angry and said that resolving the argument. Or we get committed to being right, instead of uncovering the truth. When this happens, get so wrapped up in our commitment that we can no longer see the forest through the trees. We lose touch with what we really want, because we get stuck in a mindset, and we get committed to our commitments.

(Judy- discovers a decision she made as a child and uses the discovery to transform her life and her children and grandchildren's lives).

Today, you are beginning a process that can truly change the quality of your life forever and can take that paint by numbers life you might be living now and create the masterpiece called your life. So just for a moment now, what I want you to do is imagine that your life is a painting. And imagine that you have died and are looking down at that painting. What did you leave behind? Is your life, a masterpiece that is cherished and hangs prominently as an example for others of what is possible, or is it a paint-by-numbers life that is packed away in someone's basement?

As you begin this process, I asked for only two things from you:

1. Your heartfelt desire to make real changes.
2. The commitment to follow through and do this, as simple or as located as it might seem in the moment.

If you can do just those two things, then the things that you used to call dreams will become part of your daily reality.

Why is it that you can have a person who seems to have superior abilities, talents, skills, and education, at the same time, they don't produce the quality of life they want or that you might expect from them? And why is it, on the other hand, you can have someone who seemingly has every disadvantage -- no family support, the wrong social status, no emotional support, no education, and the wrong background -- and yet they go out and produce results, way beyond what anyone could have expected or even imagined?

The difference in our quality of life is not about our capability, background or education. Human beings, *that means you*, are *all capable* of achieving incredible results, and yet sadly only a few seem to get it.

What people WILL do is very different from what people CAN do.

I want to challenge you right now to start using your WILL muscle, instead of your TRY muscle, which is probably overdeveloped anyhow. I challenge you to start exercising your inborn human power, which is your birthright as a member of the human race, your ability to act based on the choice and free will that every human has in equal measure. Frankly, this means that if it has been achieved, then there is no reason on earth why you cannot achieve it. And beyond that, if it can be imagined, then there is also very little reason why you cannot achieve it. As a matter of fact, your unconscious mind will rarely imagine something that you are capable of. That is the difference between desires and fantasies. It's true. There are no excuses anymore. If you are reading this and you are a human being that you have the ability to take action and to produce results.

The disability that I'm talking about is not something I can give you. Why? Because you already have it. You were born, great. Now, I challenge you to go out and take back what is rightfully yours.

Hopefully, something is now a weekend within you in two ways. One, by igniting your desire and two by showing you some simple systematic strategies on how you can get greater results on a daily basis.

When most of us think of success or failure, we tend to think of these monumental things. Failure is not an overnight thing, and neither is success.

Just what is success? Well, some people describe it in terms of achievements like a resume. But it is different for everyone. So, some people describe it as a feeling.

The truth is that success is wrapped up in failure. What I mean by that is that success is simply a string of failures all going in the same purposeful direction. That's right. If you want to find success you have to look inside a failure. In other words, if you want to be more successful than the next person, then you simply have to be willing to experience more failure, but not just any failures. You must be willing to take specific actions, based on specific decisions, that may fail most of the time, but keep going, perhaps with a new strategy, experience and more failures, and eventually you will succeed. If this sounds painful, then I want you to think for a moment about what true failure actually is.

True failure is lifelong failure. It is the failure of inactivity. It's not actually failing at what you DO -- those things will lead to success. But when you fail to DO, you fail to succeed. In failing to do is a recipe for ultimate failure in life. When you fail to make the calls, when you fail to follow through, when you fail to say I love you, when you fail to give your all, that is what creates the ultimate failure in life. Ultimate failure creates the greatest pain, the feelings we want to avoid at all costs. Now *that* is painful.

Success happens one step at a time. Success happens one failure at a time. It is successfully making the calls and doing it no matter how long it takes for the outcome in the moment. It is successfully getting up and following through. It is successfully making sure that you make that unique contact. It is successfully breaking through the limits that used to stop you.

Success is a combination of all those little things -- those little successes that often come disguised as failures -- over each day and over your lifetime that eventually create a life that you will have total pride and great joy in knowing that you created your life and made it into a masterpiece of your very own -- a life that is an example to others as how it is done.

The purpose of Life Masterpiece is to show you how to tap the power you were born with and how to tap into it every single day. And to make it an effortless process so that it becomes a lifestyle.

Before I go any further, I want to thank you for your friendship. Even though I have never met you, personally, I feel as if you and I are kindred spirits. The reason why say that is it you picked up this book. You made an investment. You're now reading it. This means you are one of the few who will do what others will not. This puts you light years ahead of 99% of the people. You and I encounter every day. Those people are living a paint-by-numbers life. They want to change, but they just do not get it, because they haven't got the first clue what they want and worse, they are not willing to do anything to change it.

I know you're special because you are researching and exploring and because you are reading this. It says something to me about you. It tells me that you are willing to do what it takes to succeed. It tells me that you are not satisfied with your life, and you will not be satisfied until you have successfully created your own masterpiece. So, I really want to give you the tools that can make a difference.

I have dedicated my life to understanding what makes people do what they do. What drives you? What is it that makes the difference in performance from one human being to the next? If we are all born with the same stuff, what causes some to tap into it and others to settle for a mediocre, paint-by-numbers existence?

Power comes from concentrating your focus and taking daily action to improve something. Even a 1% improvement today can result in unbelievable change, because 1% per day will not give you a 365% difference in being the year, because it builds and compounds to create a difference, way beyond anything you can probably imagine right now.

I will show you how to make it happen quickly, not 10 or 20 years from now, but today. Anything you commit to and focus on everyday must improve.

The challenge is that most of us do not know WHO we are, and therefore do not know how to control our mental focus. In fact, most of us focus on what is not working and spent most of her energy focusing on what we DON'T want by asking questions like, "how come this always happens to me?" If you focus on that enough, then that is what you will continue to experience. (Universal laws don't work unless you reprogram).

I am going to show you how to refocus your mental energy and reprogram your subconscious, so that you can ask better questions and therefore get a better result. Whatever you focus on, you manifest, which is why the Law of attraction won't work until you know what you want at the deepest level of your mind.

The key is to get you to live by those factors. Most people focus on the small stuff. I know you are to believe this, or you would not have picked up this book. Most people are so focused on what they have to DO. In other words, they focus on their to-do list, how to make a living instead of how to create their life. You could so easily get caught up in the day-to-day experiences that you tend to make a monument of the port in your mind, when actually in the long term these things that seem monumentally important now are actually quite trivial.

To create your masterpiece, you have to learn how to take care of the big things -- each color in your crayon box -- mentally, emotionally, physically, financially, and spiritually. Here are two things that usually lead to ultimate success -- either inspiration or desperation. Desperation can be a good thing because until you get really dissatisfied. You won't do anything to take your life to another level. Dissatisfaction is awesome! If you are completely satisfied, you will get comfortable. They may life begins to deteriorate.

My guess is that you invested in this book because on some level you are dissatisfied.

("If you make enough money, at least you can handle your problems in style" R)

(Lots of money, beyond comfort zone)

"It's a funny thing, the more I practice the luckier I get" AP

Subconsciously, most of us have an idea of what we think we deserve. This is our comfort zone, in which the subconscious mind determines when it sets our internal thermostat. Your subconscious mind has set your internal thermostat, and so when you begin to achieve, perhaps make a lot of money, you begin to sabotage your success dropping down to where you subconsciously think you deserve to be.

The past does not equal the future. Even if you are jaded and cynical, you've tried everything, this moment is a great new opportunity if you've tried other programs in the past that nothing has really changed your lifelong term. I believe that all it has done is it has prepared you for this program. And at some level if you did not believe that, then you would not be reading this right now.

Life Masterpiece is very different from other programs you may have tried. You will not find affirmations and visualizations and motivations in this book. What you will find is the answer to what is keeping you back, and how to reprogram your subconscious mind and how to use it to create.

Your brain is the most powerful computer on the planet. When you learn to use it properly, you can create any result you want. And they can give you the answer to almost any problem you have. The problem is that this computer, we call our brain, is not user-friendly, and does not come with an owner's manual. Life Masterpiece will show you how to operate your supercomputer with precision. Lasting change is not created in your life by learning more. Lasting change is created by using your own power to take action.

We're going to recondition the way your mind works by reprogramming your subconscious. This will change the way you feel and the way you behave for the rest of your life. Just as there have been extraordinary technological, scientific, and medical breakthroughs in the past two decades there has also been a breakthrough in the science of quantum physics. While we are not going to learn specifically about quantum physics in this book, we are going to take and use part of that technology. Because the latest cutting-edge tools for creating lasting change come from breakthroughs in quantum physics that have to do with human technology and how to get new results in record time.

There are four steps to success:

1. Know what you want. It is important for you to know what you want, and for you to know how you want things to turn out. In other words, you must know your outcome before you begin. The first step is to decide what you want out of whatever situation you are currently in. The clearer you aren't what you want, the more you will empower your brain to give you the answers.

2. You must use it. In other words, you must get yourself to take action toward your outcome. This means that you must put energy in the right direction, even when you do not know exactly what to do. Many people do not know what to do first. I will teach you exactly what to do. Some

people want to know what happens if they try, and it doesn't work. I can tell you right now, and you will learn why in this book, why nothing you try will ever work. So how do you take action? Decide to. It's not about what you can do. It's about what you will do.

3. Notice your results. It's not enough to take action. You must also pay attention to the results you are getting from your actions. Do your actions always work? No. Remember, success is just a series of failures, but failures with the purpose, failures directed at a specific result. You know what you want; you took action, now notice the result. (JS-obstacles and timing).

4. Be flexible and willing to change your approach. You must be willing to make changes and adjustments based on the results of your actions, because flexibility is the key to the system. In other words, if you notice that what you are doing is not working. And you're not getting closer to your goal or even getting further away, instead of feeling like a failure in giving up. Sometimes you simply need to change your approach.

There is a way to speed this up. Instead of just knowing what you want, taking random actions, I will show you a way to increase the pace and the certainty of your success.

("Knowledge is not power. Knowledge is potential power." R)

You may be thinking, "Jim, if this is a simple, how come everyone isn't doing it?" The answer is because the majority of people tend to get caught up in the day-to-day trivialities such as paying their bills. Now, paying your bills might seem monumentally important to you, but honestly, can you think of anyone who has ever reported that they were successful in life because they mastered the art of bill paying? I am not saying that you shouldn't pay your bills, what I'm saying is that you should know I yourself to get caught up in something trivial and make it something big, so that you can use it as an excuse for not doing the really important things in life. At the end of your life, no one is going to remember whether or not you paid all of your bills and what a wonderful job you did of it. In other words, people get caught up in making a living instead of creating a life. They come to the end of their life dissatisfied because they realize they only live 10% of it, not because they were not capable or intelligent, and not for a lack of knowledge, but simply because they never had a clear idea about what they wanted.

Some people think that what they really want is a program that deals with only one area of your life like that business program. If that is what you are thinking, let me tell you right now that Life Masterpiece is one of the most powerful business programs because it deals with the source of all your business -- YOU. When you are better will be a better speaker, salesperson negotiator. Your creativity will flow freely. Mobile to manage and influence people far more effectively than you can now. The first step to changing your career and your business is to change yourself.

***

www.lutesinternational.com

info@lutesinternational.com

https://www.facebook.com/jimluteshttps://mindmotionacademy.com

Tanja Lee

Tanja Lee is the Chief Energy Officer of The Alchemic Way, a personal development and wellness business devoted to empowering real estate leaders and teams worldwide to fulfil their potential in the least amount of time.

A multi-award-winning mentor, this once-average consumer became an industry influencer within two years and launched a global network for women in real estate.

Tanja's fresh approach and client-centric training values demonstrate her dedication to transforming the consumer experience of property from transactional and stressful to relational and memorable.

As a leadership and mindset specialist and neuro linguistic programming (NLP), practitioner Tanja has empowered thousands of people worldwide to shift their limiting beliefs, transform their self-sabotaging behaviours, and significantly grow their businesses whilst also elevating the quality of their health and happiness, relationships, and personal fulfilment.

An adventurous spirit and mother of two adult women, she has jumped out of planes, danced with Ricky Martin, meditated inside the King's Chamber of the Great Pyramid of Giza in Egypt, and lived with shamans in the jungle of Mexico.

She enjoys living in country Victoria, Australia, with her husband, Matt, and two dogs, Chief and Gilroy.

REB Mentor of the Year 2019

REB Industry Thought Leader of the Year 2019

REB Wellness Advocate of the Year 2019

Property Investment Magazine Top 10 Property Specialists of the Year 2019

Courage is The Key to Self-Empowered Change
Tanja Lee

I stood centre stage, my heart pounding in my mouth, and my black patent stiletto heels pinned to the floor by the deafening weight and soundless shock of 800 property enthusiasts who were all staring at me with a freeze-framed look of, 'What the hell just happened?' on their jaw-dropped faces.

I had just epically stuffed up on stage within the first thirty seconds of opening one of the most anticipated two-and-a-half-day property investment seminars of the year to an audience who, ten minutes earlier, raced through the heavy twelve-foot-tall mahogany doors with abundant show bags in hand, frantically filling the front seats first, as if attending their favourite sold out rock concert.

I was the emcee hired to keep the vibe high and the days flowing. My job was to introduce the respected speakers and make the paying guests feel right at home while appropriately representing the esteemed client and his brand, which was producing this life-changing financial freedom-fueled opportunity.

I failed. Horrifically. Not once, but twice, all within the first minute.

After enthusiastically welcoming everyone, I introduced myself and highlighted what an honour it was to be their emcee. Abruptly, I went completely blank. The collective excitement in the room screeched to a sudden halt as I decided that moment would be the perfect occasion to become a stand-up comedian. I tried to be funny and attempted to create a meaningful segue to the Australian Open, which was roaring with a full house just around the corner in Melbourne at the time.

No one laughed.

The silence was excruciating. My mouth, a desert, and my ears rang so loudly that I was sure the chandeliers above would shatter simultaneously with embarrassment on my behalf.

I had nothing, no raft, no notes, no comeback other than a shallow breathing squint towards the back of the overzealous carpeted ballroom where the folded-armed client stood completely discombobulated. I managed to murmur through the agonising reality, *"James, I'm so sorry, I've gone completely blank, I'm going to need you to take over."*

In addition to the sixteen hundred eyeballs now watching their own indoor grand slam, simultaneously looking at James, then back at me, then back at James, two film crews and five strategically placed video cameras captured the slow-motion car crash that happened all within a sentence.

The ballroom walls were flanked with forty attentive volunteers wearing bright citrus polo tops and matching baseball caps. The evening's esteemed speakers, whom I was supposed to respectfully introduce in the manner they would have been accustomed to, were also standing in what felt like stunned surveillance at the back of the room.

James strode towards the main stage in a super composed and considered way. He didn't acknowledge me at all. He dutifully connected with his valued clients and resuscitated the room back to his educational agenda.

I proceeded to waddle off stage awkwardly. In preparation, I bought myself a new outfit for this very important gig--A crisp white tailored shirt and a just below-the-knee black body-hugging pencil skirt with white pinstripes. I thought it would be perfect; another rookie mistake. I may have looked polished. However, it was far from practical. I ended up shuffling off the stage, a scarlet-faced Morticia. Down the stairs penguin style, one uncomfortable, long, and self-conscious step at a time.

The first keynote speaker was Matt Church, the founder and CEO of Thought Leaders. He was consistently ranked among the top ten speakers in Australia and is suitably renowned for educating people on how to turn their intellectual property into best-selling books and assisting them to become captivating international public speakers. One of the crew filming was his team. I wonder if they were and still are using my royal on-stage blunder as a perfect example of 'here's what not to do' in their speaker training programs.

James beautifully rescued the room and impressively reset the scene so that Matt could weave his lyrical magic, which he did immediately. Meanwhile, I sat shrinking at a lonely table for one on the side of the all-consuming space with a bare-fisted fight going on in the boxing ring of my mind.

In one corner, the heavyweight champion, my She-Go, was throwing all the punches. Screaming through her disapproving spittle, *"Augh YOU! Get your stuff and get out of here. No one will notice, no one cares, they'd rather you just leave. Just grab your bags and go, NOW."*

In the opposite corner, the super featherweight of my soul stood poised and softly responded, *"Ouch, okay, that must have hurt. However, you came here to do a job, Tanja, so shift your focus, listen to Masterful Matt, look for something to connect to, and get your head back in the game."*

Semi-knocked out by a defensive uppercut: *"Are you mad? I said get your gear and go. NOW. Everyone will be better off if you just left! No one wants you here. That was horrific. You're an absolute failure."*

That moment was a truly horrifying experience, other than my clothes falling off, it was the worst thing that could have publicly and professionally happened to me as an emcee with a dream to become an inspirational international speaker and for the client, well, I know that was not on the brochure.

I wanted the earth to swallow me up and spit me out at 'happy-ever-erase-that-forever-land.' However, the lessons and blessings gained from the event have been life-propelling in the theme of self-empowerment and are worthy of sharing in service of you knowing that you are not alone if you, too, fear being perceived as a failure and dread being judged like most people do, whether that's through public speaking or by any other means.

It takes something to stand up, be seen, and speak out for what we believe in. In the quest for personal and professional growth, courage—the willingness to take risks, face our fears, and walk into the unknown—is the key that unlocks possibilities for personal and professional transformation. It's not easy, but it is necessary.

I've read that most people fear speaking in public more than death, which means we would rather be in the coffin than delivering the eulogy. Yet, many of us have great things to say, ideas to share, and contributions to make, whether it be on stage, at school, in the boardroom, or in the lounge room. Still, we snuff out our self-expression and the authentic sharing of our innovations for fear of failing and avoiding receiving any form of ridicule.

So, how did this come to be? How did we each go from being a baby and a species full of love, pure potential, and promise to becoming individuals and a human race filled with fear, self-doubt, avoiding judgment, and questioning our innate value?

As a leadership and mindset coach and neuro linguistic programming (NLP) practitioner, I have had the privilege to work with thousands of people for more than three decades, and I have never met an individual who didn't doubt themselves in some way or think that they were not good enough, worthy or deserving. Whether it's a four percent or 94 percent reality, we have all had things happen in our lives that have made us decide to shrink or shy away from the heart of who we are in some minuscule or major way.

Whether our parents divorced at a young age, or perhaps we were an only child, and a sibling came along, which took the attention off us. Whether we were bullied at school or have had our hearts broken. We may have made financial mistakes and bad choices around money.

Perhaps you, too, have yoyoed with your weight, or you've had an idea bomb or a project flop. Or you've lost friendships and failed in some private or public way, it's a common yet deeply uncomfortable part of life.

Completing hundreds of personal empowerment coaching sessions over the years has taught me that it is not the unmet expectations, mistakes, and failures that cause us to hide and suffer; it's what we tell ourselves about the errors that we make that influences us the most, and not in positive ways.

Consider that when we fail, we subconsciously tell ourselves, "We're a failure," and when we get told "No," we often make it mean we're "not good enough." If our hearts get broken, we frequently decide "Don't trust women," or "Don't trust men," or "Don't give all of myself, it's not safe," and we got an answer wrong in the classroom, and the kids laughed at us, we thought "I'm dumb, never do that again."

One of the biggest contributors to our lack of self-empowerment is caused by collapsing reality with our perception of reality. We are persuaded by our limiting beliefs, not focused on the situational facts. Like motor vehicle mogul Henry Ford said, "Whether you think you can or think you can't you're right." Consider that it is not what happens to us that defines us; it's what we decide as a result.

One of my greatest mentors, best-selling author, teacher, and lecturer, Dr Joe Dispenza, shares that 98% of what we do is governed by our subconscious mind, which is full of our beliefs, judgements, opinions, and assessments of the past. His scientific research shows that we each think between sixty to ninety thousand thoughts per day; 90% of them are the same regurgitated thoughts of yesterday and decades prior, and 85% of our thinking is negative.

This means we are literally hardwiring our brains to suffer rather than succeed. Our minds and bodies say "YES" to every thought and belief we make about ourselves, others, and the world, and when most of our thinking is stinking, it has us oriented inside a victim mentality where life is negatively happening to us rather than positively for us. We hide rather than shine. We dilute our authentic self-expression and block our creative life force, which, over time, can create significant physical, emotional, mental, and spiritual impacts and even illness or disease.

It is our ego or the wounded child within, that is afraid to fail because if we fail, we risk being judged, and if we're judged, it means we may not be liked. If we're not liked, we believe we will be rejected, and if we're rejected, we'll be alone. This painful reality will only confirm our already existing belief that we are not good enough or worthy.

Even as a peak performance coach with a bounty of transformation tools, I, too, traverse my own limiting beliefs and self-sabotaging strategies. I've never met anyone who didn't have to walk through the dark woods of daunting doubts to get a glimpse of achieving the rays of radiant glory of self-empowerment and personal fulfilment.

Over the years, I have come to learn that, above all, courage is the key to self-empowered change. It requires us to hear the negative noise within and broadcast a more positive frequency. It commands us to feel the fear and do it anyway and invites us to pick ourselves up, dust ourselves off, and try again without certainty or any guarantee of a successful outcome. This takes vulnerability and is not an easy thing to do, especially when there is a boxing match in our minds, and the smelling salts of our bodies are screaming for us to avoid risk at all costs.

Not being good enough is the belief that often fuels the competitive nature of athletes, the collection of certificates from academics, and the wealth creation of entrepreneurs. It's why we see so many 'successful' people unhappy; no matter what they externally achieve or earn, it never quenches the unworthy drought within.

I've completed thousands of one-on-one coaching sessions with successful people from all walks of life, and no number of awards, public acknowledgement, certification, recognition, fame, and external gratification fills the empty pit within. This is all because we have bought into the narrative of not being good enough. The irony is that it's not what others are necessarily saying; it is what we are saying to ourselves.

Dr. David R. Hawkins, a renowned psychiatrist and spiritual teacher, is known for his influential work on consciousness, as outlined in his book "Power vs. Force." In his Map of Consciousness, Dr. Hawkins describes courage as a bridge between lower and higher emotions, serving as a vital steppingstone in the journey toward personal growth and enlightenment. Courage, in this context, plays a crucial role in transcending fear and doubt, leading us towards higher states of awareness and self-empowerment.

It requires us to be brave and demands that we go beyond the familiar and predictable territory of our mind that is flocked with the patterned wallpaper of safety, comfort, and security.

To fulfil our potential, we must learn to become comfortable with being uncomfortable because it requires us to try new things and make mistakes. American author, podcaster, and retired United States Navy officer John Cretton said, *"There is no growth in the comfort zone."* He's right; however, our ego doesn't like stuffing up and tries with all its might to block the virtues of courage in its quest to keep us swiftly protected and dutifully intact. It lacks faith and feeds on fear and comparison.

If you're like me, you too have wasted days, if not years, comparing yourself to others, questioned your ability, procrastinated, and avoided following through on your intuitive insights. You may have ignored the whispers of inspiration only to beat yourself up for doing all the above and found yourself looped in a vicious cycle of self-analysis.

You may have wished you were somewhere further than you were, however, the truth is you may not have yet done the work worthy of acknowledgement because you too were paralyzed by perfectionism. You may have even thought, like me, that others have a 'success gene' you didn't receive in the queue of life.

I believe that those who succeed are the bravehearts. They are the folk that have failed forward and failed fast. They are the ones who didn't make failure mean they were a failure.

Thomas Edison is a great example of this. I once heard a story that when Mr Edison was interviewed about how he had failed hundreds of times to perfect the light bulb his response was *"I haven't failed hundreds of times, I have eliminated hundreds of ways it does not work, in fact, I am hundreds of steps closer to the incandescent light bulb."* Imagine what would be possible if we all thought this way.

So, how can we drown out our doubt and fulfil our potential? Here are five practices of courage that, if applied, can positively propel us forward, regardless of what has happened in the past.

Be the author, not the story: We must be responsible for our limiting beliefs and self-sabotaging strategies. Responsibility means we relate to ourselves as 'able to respond' rather than negatively react. We must separate what happened from what we made it mean and avoid collapsing a negative belief into a specific situation. We must write a more empowering truth for ourselves and our future.

Ask better questions: When we are in our ego we tend to be a victim and can experience life as happening to us rather than for us. Rather than sink into emotional quicksand by asking, "Why me?"

ask, "What is this teaching me?" Pay attention to the answers and apply the learning swiftly to keep the momentum flowing.

Progress beats perfection: Consider the key to happiness is progress, not perfection. The true gift lies not in the external outcome but in who we internally become. See every setback as a divine opportunity designed to empower us to go deeper and explore further. Allow courage to be your ally on the path to committing to your dreams as you take one brave step at a time.

Replace fear with faith: There is no simulator for life and the challenges we face, much like driving a car. We learn to drive in a real car on a real road with real other cars. When it comes to setbacks, the only way through is through. Trust that the Universe or God will never give you anything you cannot handle. Replace your fear with faith and use the failures in life as fuel to courageously forge forward.

Less whip more wand: Our egos are addicted to suffering, which syphons our life source, innovations, and inspiration. That's why we must become our own champions and cheerleaders. We must focus on the efforts we are making, the lessons we are learning, and the actions we are taking and celebrate every step we make, no matter how big or small.

I don't know about you, but I want to end up at home base, sweaty and scared, having given this gift called life a red-hot crack rather than roll up to my tombstone reading – 'died with her potential intact.'

That's why I chose to muster the strength to shift my focus to Mr. Church and waddle my way back up the steps to stand before the crowd I crashed into sixty minutes prior. I chose to courageously serve rather than self-berate and wore pants the following two days.

Take a moment to consider that you are not what has happened to you; you are what you decide as a result, and you didn't come this far to come this far. You are more than enough and worthy of all the wonders of life. Don't let the pirate of your mind steal the treasure of your heart. Be the author, not the story. The stage is set for your greatness to be heard, one courageous word at a time; go speak your dreams and desires forth; the Universe is listening.

***

To contact Tanja:

Email: tanja@thealchemicway.com

Web: www.thealchemicway.com

Linkedin: thetanjalee

Instagram: @the.alchemic.way

Facebook: tanjaleeanddrmatt

Brian Blatt

Brian is a loving husband and father of two amazing (but at times, crazy) children. At the time of this publishing, he is focused on leading a world-class team to ensure the integrity and safety of ExxonMobil's North American pipelines. Outside of the office, he has authored Lessons from the Breakfast Table (a must-read for all who wish to grow) and, along with his brother-in-law, creates private placement opportunities in cash flow-producing multi-family residential properties.

Brian benefited from a strong family environment where lessons of success were taught daily. In Brian's younger years, he and his older brother and sister spent six years delivering the morning newspaper seven days a week. This ingrained discipline and work ethic began when Brian was 8 years old. Additionally, the paper route instilled a financial mindset, as all income was invested and would later pay for much of his Ohio State University education, where Brian received a Bachelor of Science in Mechanical Engineering with Cum Laude recognition.

Before Brian joined the workforce, where he later earned his Master of Business Administration from the University of Houston, Brian drawled upon the keys of success and obtained his pilot's license. He also applied the principles of success to sports in his younger years, where he was a high school four-sport letterman, All-State football player, and a division 1 walk-on for WVU.

Breaking Through the Invisible Barrier of FEAR

By Brian Blatt

My hope with this chapter is to provide some inspiration and help you take action despite fear's best attempts at holding you hostage. If any of the following sounds preachy, note that this is written out of love for my children, and God willing, someday their children. But mostly, the lecturing is directed at myself.

What if you could not fail at any endeavor? What would you go for in life if you were guaranteed to succeed? What vision comes to mind? Where would you live? What would you drive? With whom would you be friends? Where would you travel? How often would you travel? What charities would you begin? What would you be doing? And most importantly, who would you become?

I've come to realize that the playbook for creating the life you dream of is not that complicated. It might not always be easy, but it's not complicated. And while there is no silver bullet to achieving success, there are golden BBs. I'm convinced that there are keys that, if taken to heart and applied consistently over time, will place you on a trajectory to reach any goal. And the question will not be "if" you will achieve your goals, but a matter of "when".

And the crazy thing is the keys are not mysterious and do not require skill to implement. In fact, that is why in my book, Lessons from the Breakfast Table, Keys to Success from A to Z, I intentionally wrote it so a child could read. And while the lessons are taught through simple stories and analogies so children can understand, the meaning and applicability resonate profoundly with leaders and achievers at every level.

In fact, I bet you can guess several of the keys… A is for Attitude, B is for Believe, C is for Choice, and D is for Dream to name a few. You can look to any top performer, and I'd bet you a steak dinner that they apply the principles from A to Z far better than the masses.

So, then the curious question that I think about is, if the playbook for achieving success is frankly straight forward, why then are so few people planting and nurturing more seeds of success? The fact that you are reading this book tells me you are one of the few who seek out good information and are actively working on growth. Likely many of you have read the classic self-development books from the likes of Napolean Hill, Earl Nightingale, Jim Rohn, Les Brown, Jim Britt, Jim Lutes, Tony Robbins and Ed Mylett to name a few. Additionally, within the pages of this book, there is no doubt that my fellow co-authors have offered several strategies, tactics, and systems that if applied, are sure to take you to the next level.

Knowledge of the ages is available to us all. Seeking information and continuously learning is important, but without action, the knowledge alone is no more valuable than trivia shared at the bar.

Let's turn our attention to the elephant in the room and reflect on the number one obstacle that is holding us all back (me included), and that is FEAR. Over the next several pages, I hope to provide a perspective on the deceitful chameleon and provide ways to handle and ultimately overcome fear in pursuit of your goals and dreams and ultimately becoming a better version of yourself.

So, you have doubts, concerns and questions… great! That is normal and is an indication that you are embarking on an opportunity for growth. People might laugh at you… excellent! First of all, people are not thinking about you; they are thinking about themselves. But even if they were talking about you, it is because you are doing something different than the masses. Becoming the best version of yourself and achieving more than others requires you to do things differently. Let the weak-minded talk and gossip. Don't arrive at your deathbed with regrets of not going for your dreams because of what you thought other people would think.

When I was approached with the opportunity to be a contributing co-author in this book, I must confess, the voice of fear started to make a ruckus. The fear puppet had me asking myself questions such as, "Had I achieved enough to be a credible contributing co-author? Was I good enough? What would I write about?" The fear puppet then reminded me that we had some upcoming home improvement projects, so the investment was not the right time. Additionally, I was in the middle of an equity raise with my brother in-law where we are building apartment properties and just the week prior, a $500k commitment dried up! The fear puppet is a sneaky chameleon and often disguises itself as a voice of reason.

So, as I sat down at the computer to email Mr. Britt to let him know that I would have to pass on this incredible opportunity, I knew the reasons that I was typing were all excuses and were based out of fear. In these moments of reflection, when I feel I'm at the crossroads of fear and growth, I ask myself, "Would the person I aspire to become proceed forward with this kind of endeavor?" And when I think of the person, I want to become ten years from now, that person absolutely would have figured out a way to lean into this opportunity while moving forward with his real estate syndication and all the other family and work responsibilities. This thought process provided me with the courage and calmness to press forward and softened the voice of fear. Fortunately, what began as an apologetic decline to Mr. Britt ended with me accepting the invitation and clarifying the message I was to write about in this book.

Fear is normal. Fear speaks up prior to a moment of growth and is an indicator that you are on the right path. Ask yourself if the future better version of yourself would have been likely to take action. If the answer is most definitely, then there you have it, proceed forward. Now this won't guarantee that the outcome will immediately succeed. But if it doesn't, so what, you learned something and you proved to yourself that you are one of the brave ones that move forward despite the discouragement of fear. Besides, it's not the momentary mistakes and failures that prevent success, rather, it's the inaction caused by fear that prevents growth and success. As Michael Jordan said, "You miss 100% of the shots that you don't take."

Here's a short story that might provide a different way of looking at and overcoming fear.

When my youngest sister Sarah was around five years old, I would have been thirteen and full of wisdom (insert laugh). At night, I'd go into her room and tell her stories before bedtime. And often, it would be a ghost story (I know, a real teenage butthead). The moment I said the word "ghost" or such and such "died", she would scream and run to our parents.

One night as I was talking to Sarah, I told her that she shouldn't be afraid of nightmares. I explained that while she might be having the scariest nightmare, in reality, she was laying comfortably in bed under her covers. Nightmares were nothing more than her imagination playing a movie. But again, no matter how scary the movie was, the reality was she was safe and sound.

From that moment on, she was no longer afraid of my bedtime stories. In fact, later in life she told me that she remembers asking for nightmares during her bedtime prayers! Okay, I'm not sure I'd go that far, but the point is, as a five-year-old, she understood her imagination and began to reduce its ability to produce fear. When I feel fear raising its head, I will tell myself that while the voice and feelings of fear are uncomfortable, in reality, it's analogous to a bad dream, and taking action is the best way to assure myself that I'm safe and sound under my covers on the path towards success.

And for Sarah, her commitment to outworking the masses and taking massive action has always been her trademark. She held multiple track and cross-country records for her high school. She graduated from the United States Coast Guard Academy and is currently piloting helicopters as a Lieutenant Commander. And for kicks, she completed the Falcon 50 which is a 50-mile race in Colorado open to all Academy graduates where she set the women's record by nearly an hour!

I share these accomplishments as a proud big brother, partly to brag, but mostly to provide a story that illustrates how if you can prioritize work and action over imagined FEAR, you'll be amazed at what you can achieve. And the good news is that as soon as you begin taking action, the fear subdues. The sneaky voice tries everything it can to prevent you from taking action, but once you begin, it's as if it said, "well, I tried" and goes away.

Another way I'd like to suggest on how to combat the voice of fear is to fill your mind with great thoughts, ideas and messages from the great leaders and achievers. Regardless of which endeavor you are pursuing; likely it has already been accomplished. Furthermore, there is probably a book, YouTube video and/or Podcast that dives into the specific strategy and tactics used to achieve the outcome. I find the more stories I fill my mind with, the better I'm able to quiet the voice of fear. When I'm debating on whether to pursue some venture, it is extremely helpful to be able to reflect on the countless messages from those who have gone before me. For instance, I think, "How would Abraham Lincoln respond to this setback? What would Jim Rohn say about my level of activity? What would Zig Ziglar's outlook be?" And perhaps, the most calming message I go back to in a moment of doubt is what the greatest Teacher of all said, "Ask, and it will be given to you; seek, and you will find; knock, and it will be opened to you."

For both my Jewish and Christian friends, the number one message that is mentioned over and over throughout both the Hebrew and Christian bibles is "be not afraid", "have no fear", and "fear not". I could be wrong, but I believe that God knows fear is what will hold us back from becoming the greatest version of ourselves. This is why he has spoken some version of "be not afraid" through the angels, prophets and through Jesus himself so many times.

Let me offer a final secular example of how acting despite fear has proven to be very valuable. I referenced the real estate syndication previously. Prior to combining efforts with my brother in-law, Daryl and scaling up multi-family residential apartments, I began with my very first rental property. At the time of my first closing, I was nervous and scared. The puppet of fear would have been better described as a dragon of fear. All the typical thoughts were racing through my mind. "What if I couldn't find a tenant? What if I get expensive damages? How much time will this require? I don't like fixing broken appliances. Will I be getting calls in the middle of the night?"

There was so much I didn't know then, but looking back, I am extremely proud of my younger self for acting despite the fear. I knew no matter how many books I read or people I talked to, the only way I was going to move forward was by taking action in spite of the fear. And while each of the next 22 closings since have garnered my full attention, the voice of fear has greatly been diminished.

You can quiet fear through study and preparation, but the only way to muzzle fear is through experience. Growth requires taking action beyond our comfort zones. But once we've done that, we have just expanded our comfort zone and increased the experiences and memories that we will be able to create from this precious life.

And while there has certainly been some active time spent learning and managing this asset class, the knowledge I've gained, the people I've met, and yes, the money I've made have all more than made up for any of the challenging times faced along the way.

Summing it up:

- Fear is normal and an indicator of an opportunity for growth.
- Fear is sneaky and can sound a lot like sound reason.
- Fear's objective is to keep you safe exactly where you are. However, this is also the antithesis of growth.
- Tips for overcoming fear and taking action include:
    - Ask yourself if the person you aspire to become 10 years from now would likely have moved forward with the activity. If the answer is "absolutely", move forward. Take a step closer to becoming the person you aspire to be.
    - Think of fear as a bad dream. Despite how terrible the nightmare is, know that in reality, you are safe and sound under the covers. Fear can stir your emotions but know the path to success requires moving forward. And the more you become, the safer you are.
    - Fill your mind with lessons from great leaders and achievers from all walks of life. When you find yourself at the crossroads met with fear, the messages and stories from those who have gone before you will provide ammunition to fend off fear.
    - Jewish and Christians alike, remember that God has given some version of the message "be not afraid" more than any other message throughout the holy scriptures. It must be important.
    - Study and preparation do help quiet fear, but the best way to muzzle fear is through experience. Take action, that is the only way that growth can occur.

I'm grateful you invested your time with me during this chapter and genuinely hope that this was worthwhile and helpful to you as you pursue your dreams and goals. If reflecting on any of the stories and messages helps get you over a moment of fear and take action, this will undoubtedly have been worth it. Because in the end, nothing is achieved without taking action. And a single action can be the very spark that ignites you and others into a blazing movement of accomplishments making this world a better place.

Lastly, in case you are wondering, yes, there was a principle dedicated to addressing fear in my book, Lessons from the Breakfast Table… V is for Valor.

Be great!

***

To contact Brian:

Phone: 214-548-9767

Email: blatt.20@gmail.com

LinkedIn profile: https://www.linkedin.com/in/brian-blatt-42766839/

Instagram profile: https://www.instagram.com/blatt.brian/

Lessons from the Breakfast Table: Available online through Amazon, Barnes & Noble and Balboa Press

https://firethorn-capital.com – If interested in learning more about real estate project opportunities

Cyndy Violette

Cyndy Violette is a professional poker player known for her success in live tournaments, online tournaments, and live cash games. Born in August 1959, she began playing poker in the early 1980's when poker was said to be a man's game. She achieved much success and quickly made a name for herself in the high stakes world of poker. Violette has won several major tournaments, including a World Series of Poker (WSOP) bracelet in 2004. She is respected for her strategic gameplay and positive mindset and has been a prominent figure in the poker community for decades.

The Life of a Poker Legend

By Cyndy Violette

My history and Legacy in the high stakes world of poker

Let me give you a brief history on how I discovered my passion for the game of poker. I was born in Queens, New York, lived there until the age of 12, and then my family decided to move to Las Vegas. I went to jr. high, high school, and 1 year of college. I was going to school to become an emergency medical technician until it was interrupted by a major car accident. I had a broken jaw and during that time I met my husband, Rod; I was 21 years old at the time.

My family life growing up was somewhat "normal". My mom was a hostess at the Tropicana casino, and my dad was an entertainer, maître de, and owned a very successful nightclub. My dad was never into poker, but he did run crap games in the basement of his night club and he loved to bet on sports. I can remember during football season on Sundays, dad, mom and I always watched football together, made great Italian dinners, and we made bets on the games. We had a lot of fun. Those were some great family memories. My dad was my biggest poker fan and was always there watching me on many final tables. He was very proud of me.

I was pregnant with my daughter Shannon when I started playing poker. I was on pregnancy leave from my job at the time. I was a blackjack dealer at the famous Binion's HorseShoe casino in Las Vegas. I ended up getting a divorce and became a single mom. This is when I fell in love with the game. It was in the early 80's when poker was still considered a man's game. At the time there were only a few women really playing, and I was usually the only female playing at the table. Being a pioneer, I helped pave the way for other women to start playing poker. Now there are a lot more women players, and many are very good and successful.

I decided to take the leap and play poker full time. I started out playing in small games and tournaments around town to hone my skills, as I got better and better. As I progressed, I played in many major tournaments. At that time there were not a lot of poker books or information from poker experts available, so it was a lot of trial and error. The first major tournament I won was in 1986 at the Grand Prix at the Golden Nugget casino, with a first-place prize of $74,000. At the time it was the most ever won by a woman. I always play in the World Series of Poker and I'm very proud to say I have a WSOP Bracelet: I won in 2004 in the 7-card stud 8 or better event, with 1st place of $139,000. I have made many other final tables and several tournament cashes to date. I have played events in the televised World Poker Tour, and was on a few other Poker TV shows, such as Poker Royalty, Super Stars of Poker on Fox Network, other WSOP events on ESPN, and NBC heads up matches.

It was a great honor to be inducted into the prestigious Women's Poker Hall of Fame in 2008.

My poker career has given me the opportunity to travel the world over, playing in tournaments and live cash games. In 1994 I moved to Atlantic City, NJ for ten years when they first legalized poker. This was an ideal time for poker: it was during the "poker boom" and poker was just starting to become very popular, and people were just learning the game. We had some of the best high stakes poker cash games on the weekends at the Trump Taj Mahal. These 10 years were some of my most memorable. It was a great time in life. I only played poker on weekends and my friends always knew once Friday rolled around, I was usually not available until Monday.

It was a great balance. I always had the weekdays to enjoy time with my friends and family. I used to have many parties and health related events at my beautiful home in Galloway, NJ. My home had a lagoon pool, fishpond, lush landscaping and a yard that looked like a resort hotel. I've always been passionate about designing and decorating.

The lifestyle of a poker player, besides being a lot of hard work it has had its ups and downs. It definitely has its pluses. The best plus is being my own boss. One of the things I love is that I meet so many great and interesting people from all walks of life and play poker with many celebrities. I have traveled all over the world and stayed in some of nicest casino resorts and spas. In poker you can play and quit whenever you want, so you're in control of your own schedule and your own destiny.

What makes a Poker Champion, both on and off the table

One of my key qualities is my ability to remain calm and focused under pressure in the high-pressure environment of tournaments and high-stake cash games. Maintaining emotional stability is essential and has helped me weather the ups and downs of the game and emerge victorious time and time again.

Poker really begins away from the table. How you prepare and how you feel before you even sit at the table. Playing your best poker requires a lot of different ingredients. Anyone can learn the actual game, but keeping a clear mind and maintaining a good attitude is essential. When I lose a pot, I don't let it get to me, I let it go. I don't complain or show any emotions. It's all part of the game. Poker is about the big picture and the long run. This is just as important as poker strategies and technical things like starting hands, pot odds, and value bets. So, before I even consider going to play, first of all I make sure I get a good sleep so I'm well rested. A good sleep will definitely affect how you react and be ready to play some long hours if needed. What I eat is very important to me. I'm vegan and love good healthy organic food and I cook a lot. I pack up food to take with me, and back in the day I even had personal chefs cook for me and bring me my meals to the table.

I always take time to pray and meditate. Before I get in the shower it is very important to me to treadmill to get my energy flowing and listen to something positive and motivating. I visualize how my day is going to go and clear any blocks that I might have to winning. I also work on getting in alignment and focusing on my goals. When you feel great, you're going to make better decisions. I really enjoy taking care of myself and my favorite is getting massages. These are some of the things that will make me better and give me the edge over my opponents. For me preparation has been the key and foundation of being successful!

When I first get into the poker game, I study the players and feel the vibe in the game, see who is winning and who is losing, and see if anyone is on tilt. Even if you know the players from previous games, their circumstances can change and affect the way they play. Are they playing their "A game" or their "D game" today? Some people play totally differently if they're winning or losing. It's always important to observe those factors before getting too involved and just relying on their past play.

The less that I have on my mind while I'm playing the better. That makes it easier to get in the zone, stay in the zone, and maintain focus. The fewer distractions the better. It takes a lot more discipline these days not to be on your cell phones too much; they always seem to be demanding your attention. One text, phone call, or social media post can totally shift your mood and focus. Staying centered and in the moment is crucial. Being a winning poker player takes a combination of lots of ingredients: dedication, discipline, determination, patience, and bankroll management, among others.

While I'm at the table, I'll take breaks and check in with myself to see if I'm still as focused and playing as well as I could be. I have always said that poker mirrors life. So, what happens if I don't prepare or let outside issues creep in? How I'm doing in the game is usually a direct reflection of my inner self getting mirrored back to me in the cards. When I'm not doing well at the table, it's usually when I have something in life bothering me or on my mind. I feel blocked. I like to take breaks and change up the energy and work on clearing it. When I go in fully prepared and feeling great, I know my chances of having a great session are way better. I love when I feel unstoppable, and I know I'm going to win!

Poker can be very unforgiving when you're not prepared.

This is why it's really about knowing yourself. There is no automatic paycheck for just putting in your time: you have to win to get paid. That's what I love about poker: It keeps you always working on yourself! So, my poker career has been an amazing challenging life.

Pursuing my Dreams beyond Poker

I played poker for about 30 years and then ventured on a long-time vision of mine. I became vegan in the early 90's and always dreamed of opening a vegan organic restaurant. My calling finally did come to fruition with a blessing from God in 2015 and Violette's Vegan restaurant was born. It was a very popular and beautiful restaurant. So, during that time I was focusing on business, and I was not playing as much poker. I had the restaurant for over 7 years, but sadly, after covid we ended up having to close it.

After my few years hiatus from playing serious high stakes poker, I'm excited to get back in the game and resharpen my poker mindset, focus, clarity, and skills. I'm gearing up now and getting ready for more success on the green felt.

***

To contact Cyndy:

https://www.facebook.com/cyndyviolette

Brian Hite

Brian Hite is a modern-day Renaissance man, masterfully blending high-octane stunt work with intellectual rigor and the transformative power of sport/performance psychology. Boasting over 130 film and TV credits, including a prestigious Screen Actors Guild award for "24," Brian brings a rich tapestry of experiences to every new endeavor.

Holding a Master's in Sport Psychology, a Ph.D. in Organizational Psychology, and certified as a Mental Performance Consultant (CMPC), Brian is a recognized authority on human potential. His expertise is sought after by the U.S. Army for peak performance strategies and doctoral candidates at Grand Canyon University whom he mentors.

As founder of Brian Hite Global, Brian captivates audiences with electrifying storytelling and actionable insights. His keynote addresses transcend industries, offering fresh perspectives on resilience, adaptation, risk-taking, and flourishing during challenging times.

An enthusiastic experiencer of life, Brian is just as happy flying through the air on his dirt bike as he is at a Broadway show. His infectious passion inspires others to embrace the unknown and push beyond limits. A published author, his book "Begin Again" blends ancient wisdom with modern practicality, while two additional books (coming soon) target mental strength for entrepreneurs.

In a world requiring physical and mental resilience, Brian Hite stands as a beacon of inspiration, reminding us that our overall wellbeing emerges from embracing life's journey with courage and curiosity.

Begin Again:
Mastering the Art of Resilience
By Brian C. Hite

"Cut on rehearsal!"

I vaguely remember hearing these words as I lay on the ground, trying to piece together what had just happened. I knew I was lying next to the motorcycle I'd been riding, but how I ended up on the ground the way I did was still fuzzy.

I remembered hearing "Action on rehearsal!" and riding the motorcycle through the double doors of a building, down some concrete stairs, across the sidewalk, off the curb, and into the street. I remembered locking up the back brake and starting to slide a 90, thinking I was going a little too fast. I remembered feathering the front brake to control the speed and distance of the slide, and then, suddenly, I was on the ground.

I had a few scrapes and bruises here and there, but nothing that needed immediate attention. The motorcycle, however, was missing quite a few pieces and, most importantly, refused to start. That was a big problem because the next thing up was the shot we'd been rehearsing when I wrecked. Without the motorcycle, we couldn't do the shot, and we had to do the shot.

The big irony was that the scripted end of the rehearsed shot involved me wrecking the motorcycle. In addition to being a sports/performance psychologist, I'm also a stuntman. On this particular episode of Hawaii Five-O, I'd been hired to double an actor trying to escape on a motorcycle. The action was supposed to be exactly as I described above, but instead of ending with the motorcycle and me lying on the pavement, I was supposed to crash in a way that put the motorcycle and myself in the grass.

Now, however, because the motorcycle wouldn't work, we couldn't do that shot. The stunt coordinator and producer were mad. But as angry as they were (and they were *livid*), the intensity of their emotions paled in comparison to the intensity of my complex cornucopia of thoughts and feelings. My emotions careened at light speed among frustration, anger, embarrassment, disappointment, and fear.

At that moment following the rehearsal, I was the center of attention, trapped in a spotlight that exposed my flaws and illuminated my failure. And, unlike other times when I've felt the same way, my perception that everybody was looking at me and talking about me was not the result of an overactive ego. There was no hiding from the fact that I was the subject of every discussion on that set.

Because the motorcycle couldn't be fixed, the decision was made to push the shot to the next day and to move on with the rest of their shot list, at which point I was effectively forgotten. On its surface, this shift in everyone's attention might seem like a good thing. However, what it *actually* did was remove everything distracting me, even slightly, from my thoughts and emotions.

Finding a place to be alone when working on a show can be challenging, but I found a place away from everybody else where I could stew in isolation. This was my first mistake (well, second mistake). Then, I replayed the wreck over and over in my mind. This was my next mistake.

For the next hour or two, I alternated between sitting and pacing back and forth while excoriating myself in the most brutal ways possible for the mistake I'd made. The cognitive and emotional vortex did not subside but grew and strengthened to unbelievable proportions.

I wanted so badly to get back on the motorcycle and do the stunt correctly, to give the stunt coordinator, producer, and director the shot they wanted, and to show the rest of the crew that I actually could do the stunt in a way that both looked good and was safe for all involved.

But I had to wait, isolated physically but accompanied constantly by swirling, powerful thoughts and emotions that refused to weaken. I knew I needed to let go of what had happened and focus, instead, on the future, on what needed to be done the next time I found myself on the motorcycle, the next time I heard, "Action!" I knew I needed to reset myself, but how?

How could I let go of what had happened? How could I just start over? All I wanted to do was Begin Again.

***

Every one of us has experienced moments when we simply wanted to push a reset button when we'd give anything to delete the memories and erase the consequences of our actions.

Although going back in time is not possible (yet), it *is* possible to Begin Again. It *is* possible to allow the past to be the past and the future to unfold as it will. It *is* possible to ground ourselves in the only moment that is real, the only moment that truly exists, and make the best choices we can.

That moment is the present.

So, how do we do it? How do we let go of what was and what we believe *might* be to Begin Again completely anew in this present moment?

By developing self-awareness, acceptance, and self-regulation.

These three skills, and they are skills, are the keys to continually progressing in ways that utilize experiences from the past, leverage our visions and hope for the future, and maintain a realistic connection to the present moment, the only moment when we can affect change.

As I said, self-awareness, acceptance, and self-regulation are skills, meaning that just like anything else you used to be unable to do but now can, these skills can be learned and continually improved. So, throughout the rest of this chapter, I'll discuss how they can be developed and why they are helpful.

Self-Awareness

Because it is impossible to accept or change something if we aren't aware that that "something" is a problem, beginning again must start with self-awareness. Cultivating the ability to tune into our thoughts, emotions, moods, and behaviors is the first step to letting go of what was and beginning again in the present moment.

As mentioned above, self-awareness encompasses thoughts, emotions, and behaviors, both in the moment as well as existing patterns that have developed over time. It refers to ephemeral, short-lived emotions and to moods that persist for longer periods. It refers to heat-of-the-moment thoughts and to core beliefs that follow us from situation to situation. It refers to knowledge of what we are doing each moment, our deliberate actions, our knee-jerk reactions, the way we communicate and interact with others, and to patterns of behavior that may have become so habitual that we are rarely aware they are happening at all.

And ultimately, self-awareness involves understanding the connections and interactions among thoughts, moods, emotions, and actions.

Enhancing Self-Awareness

1. Take a snapshot of your current state at regularly scheduled times throughout the day.

This might be upon waking, when transitioning from one task to another, or just prior to a particular activity. For example, as soon as we wake up, we can perform a body scan to take stock of exactly how our bodies feel, how rested we feel, and how much energy we have. We can tune into our overall mood, thoughts, emotions, and complex interplay among all three.

We can also conduct this same check-in before/after lunch, before/after meetings, and when transitioning from "work mode" to "home mode." Whatever our schedules, we all benefit from regularly scheduled attention to our physical, mental, and emotional states.

2. Pay particular attention during specific moments in time when thoughts are racing, emotions are powerful, or actions have important consequences.

Most of our lives are not spent in a high-arousal state. Most of the time, we roll peacefully and calmly from one moment to the next. However, there are times when energy and engagement levels are higher than usual. These might be times when there is something we really value at stake, a time crunch, or a feeling of being overwhelmed. Maybe it's an important conversation with a spouse or child, running late while trying to get to a meeting, or juggling cooking, cleaning, and homework help all at the same time.

The powerful thoughts and emotions we experience during these moments should serve as indicators, red flags, that we must tune in more closely to ourselves. They are perfect times to fully bring our thoughts, emotions, and actions into our conscious awareness by "stepping outside" of ourselves to examine our thoughts and feelings as thoroughly and objectively as possible. In this way, we can avoid being carried down the rabbit hole by our fleeting and reactionary thoughts and feelings.

3. Reflect

Although cultivating awareness of our moment-to-moment states is essential, we often miss important things that can only be perceived and understood retrospectively. When emotions are strong and energy activation levels are high, our attention tends to narrow, and our ability to think broadly and creatively, to synthesize and evaluate all of the information coming in becomes compromised. Later reflection, however, can:

Illuminate important aspects of our situations that we missed while caught in the maelstrom of earlier events.

Help us better understand what truly happened at that particular point in time.

Guide our perceptions and choices in the future.

Reflection can happen at any time, but I recommend reflecting at the beginning and end of the day. Reflection in the morning allows us to think through our upcoming day to 1) set intentions for how we want to be and 2) decide how to apply strategies and lessons learned from the past. For example, suppose we know that one kid needs to go to soccer and another needs to be picked up from gymnastics. In that case, we can use this morning reflection time to gain clarity about how we want to be during that busy time (e.g., patient, kind) and to identify techniques we can use to eliminate, or at least mitigate, some of the stress and tension we're likely to feel.

Reflecting in the evening allows us to examine the day from a place of calm and equanimity that is difficult to achieve in the heat of the moment. This look back on our day can provide valuable insight into things that went well and things that didn't, hopefully increasing the likelihood of the former and decreasing the likelihood of the latter.

For example, a meltdown (by either you or your child) may have occurred during homework. In the moment, you saw the situation in one way and responded accordingly. However, upon reflection, you might see that situation differently and revise your thoughts about how you handled yourself based on that new understanding.

It is impossible to change something if we don't know it needs changing. Self-awareness is critical because knowledge of what's going on physically, mentally, emotionally, and socially is required to take any productive steps in our desired direction. However, simple awareness of our circumstances is not enough. We must also accurately and thoroughly understand our circumstances and accept things as they truly are. For this, we need the skill of acceptance.

Acceptance

Once we become aware of thoughts, emotions, behaviors, and moods, we must accept them just as they are. It's important to remember, though, that "acceptance" in this sense is not synonymous with acquiescence or resignation. It doesn't mean we simply concede that the way things are now is the way they will always be. On the contrary, once we become aware of our current state, acceptance is the thing that allows for meaningful change to occur.

The alternative to acceptance is to deny that our thoughts, emotions, and actions are what they are and impact us and those we care about in the way they do. The alternative to acceptance is a world of excuses and rationalizations that result in perpetual disconnection from what's happening with ourselves and those around us. And this causes all kinds of problems.

Accepting our circumstances means acknowledging reality in the present moment exactly as it is. We might like it, or we might hate it. However, regardless of our feelings about whether we want things to change or to stay the same, we accept how things truly are right now because that is the only way to develop an accurate and thorough enough understanding of what's going on for us to do anything about it.

For example, imagine your spouse agreeing to cook dinner, but you walk in the door from transporting kids hither and yon to find the kitchen in the same condition as when you left the house. Anger and frustration are immediately felt, and the desire to find and castigate your spouse for their unholy transgression as soon as humanly possible is almost overpowering.

Because you read the previous section on self-awareness, though, you take the time to bring your thoughts and feelings into full awareness. When you do, you recognize the powerful emotions and the aggressive thoughts driving those emotions and the physical changes that occurred (e.g., increased heart rate, rapid and shallow breathing, and muscle tension).

This awareness is critical and necessary for navigating the situation as well as possible, but it is insufficient. You must also accept the truth and reality of what you think and feel, even if they're not what you'd like to think and feel. This may seem straightforward and obvious, but it can sometimes be challenging.

For example, maybe you've been taught that being mad at your spouse is bad. Maybe you've learned, explicitly or implicitly, that confrontation is an evil that must be avoided at all costs. As a result, you might be aware of your physical, mental, and emotional states but resist acknowledging or accepting them for what they are. You might try to convince yourself that you don't feel as angry as you actually do or that the absence of dinner is somehow your fault.

If, however, you accept that your thoughts, emotions, and physiological conditions are what they are - simply acknowledge the reality of the present moment - it's possible for control to be gained and meaningful, productive steps to be taken.

So, awareness is not enough. We must also accept our present moment reality precisely as it is. Again, this doesn't mean that we necessarily believe that our circumstances are okay or resign ourselves to dealing with our issues for time immemorial. It simply means that we let go of resistance and stop trying to fight against what is. Once we've done that and accepted our reality, we can change things we'd like to be different or sustain things we'd like to keep.

That is, we can use self-regulation.

Self-Regulation

Self-regulation refers to anything we do to intentionally manage our thoughts, behaviors, and actions. If things are going well, self-regulation strategies maintain the status quo. If things are not going well, self-regulation strategies target the issues contributing to the undesirable state. Either way, the moment we engage in self-regulation is the same moment we Begin Again.

Human beings are a complex web of physical, mental, emotional, and social components operating synergistically from moment to moment. Therefore, the most beneficial self-regulation strategies impact all of those components comprehensively and coordinatedly. There are myriad ways to self-regulate, so a comprehensive discussion of all of them (if that were even possible) is beyond the scope of this chapter. However, I will present two strategies that can be put to use immediately and in a broad range of situations.

Breathing

One of the simplest and most widely applicable self-regulation strategies is breathing. This seems like a stupid thing to call a "strategy" because it's a requirement for life and (since you're reading this) clearly something you do proficiently. However, the simple acts of taking in mostly oxygen and expelling mostly carbon dioxide are not what we mean when discussing breathing as a self-regulation strategy. Breathing to self-regulate involves using certain techniques that can be adjusted depending on our needs.

For example, if we realize we are too amped up and feel overly nervous, anxious, fearful, or excited, breathing rhythmically from the diaphragm can help us regulate the effects of those emotions. On the other hand, if we realize we are sluggish and our energy activation level is too low, we can breathe deeply and a little more quickly. This activates the sympathetic nervous system (Fight or Flight) and, in turn, initiates physiological changes that result in immediate energy boosts.

Simply tuning into and becoming aware of the breath can also be helpful. As human beings, we can't pay attention to everything at once. So, when we become overwhelmed by the sheer volume of things competing for our attention, shifting our complete attention to our breath reduces the turbulence of our minds and emotions, which puts us in a much better position to reset and Begin Again.

So, regardless of whether we're overly amped, not amped enough, or just have too many thoughts and emotions whirling and churning, engaging in rhythmic, purposeful breathing helps us regain control of our minds and bodies in a way that allows us to Begin Again.

Taking control of the body through breathing is a terrific first step to any attempt to begin again and can be used in conjunction with this next strategy, reframing.

Reframing

Reframing is an incredibly powerful strategy that allows us to mold and shape reality in whatever way we want simply by changing how we think about it. You might say, "That's impossible. Reality is reality; what is, just is. How can my thoughts about reality possibly change reality?"

As Stoic philosophers like Epictetus and Marcus Aurelius remind us, how we understand our world directly results from the meanings we assign to the things that happen to us. Shakespeare's Hamlet voices this truth clearly and succinctly when he states, "Nothing is either good or bad but thinking makes it so." Things that happen to us, by themselves, are neither good nor bad. Our perception of these things, the way we think about them, makes them good or bad.

Reframing is purposely altering our perception of events in ways that highlight the benefits or usefulness of those events. The situation itself doesn't change at all. However, how we *think* about the situation and the way we *understand* what's going on changes in helpful and productive ways. Reframing might involve switching our attention from one thing to another, reprioritizing aspects of our circumstances, or going completely outside the box and viewing things differently and from points of view we've never considered before.

For example, if we find ourselves stuck in traffic, we might become aware that we're irritated and frustrated. These emotions manifest when we believe we are being harmed in some way or when we believe people are doing something wrong. In this particular case, we think the other people on the road are harming us by keeping us from getting where we want to go.

If we were to reframe the situation, however, we might shift our focus away from what we are being prevented from doing (making progress toward our destination) to what we are afforded the opportunity to do. This might include having the time to listen to an audiobook or podcast, make phone calls, broach important topics of conversation with our kids, or simply enjoy some all-too-rare alone time.

When we shift our attention from what we believe we're missing to what we believe we are receiving, our entire attitude and outlook on the situation changes. Frustration and irritation transform immediately into joy and gratitude, and this transformation occurs with no change at all to our circumstances, only to how we think about our circumstances.

Once we've developed awareness and accepted the true nature of our current and past circumstances, we can take tangible, concrete steps to self-regulate. We might adjust our thoughts, cultivate specific emotions, alter our mood, change our behaviors, or, most likely, employ some combination of all four. Regardless of which self-regulation strategies we choose, as long as those strategies are grounded in the wisdom we've gained through self-awareness and acceptance, we can be relatively certain we've set ourselves up for success each time we Begin Again.

Conclusion

All of us have moments that disrupt our Zen, that screw up our equilibrium, and demolish our overall well-being. In these moments, we often wallow in what was or worry about what might be. However, this fixation on the past and future doesn't help us at all because we end up spending all of our energy beating ourselves up over something in the past that, by definition, can't be changed or worrying incessantly about something in the future that, also by definition, isn't real. As a result, our obsession and preoccupation with the past and future prevent us from putting our energies into the only time and place we can affect the present.

So, the next time you find yourself in a challenging situation, Begin Again.

Use the amazing power of self-awareness to accurately and unambiguously identify your physical, mental, and emotional states. Then, stop fighting or resisting these conditions and accept your current reality. Lastly, with the knowledge gained from these first two steps, develop a self-regulation plan that addresses your physical, mental, and emotional condition in ways that allow you to let go of what *was* and what you believe *might be* and focus instead on what *is*…so you can Begin Again.

[Unfortunately, due to space, this chapter was edited in a way that resulted in the culmination of the story being cut. However, if you'd like to know how the story ends…how the techniques described in the chapter were applied and how the stunt went the next day…you can have access to the full, unedited chapter for free here: www.BrianHiteGlobal/BonusContent]

***

To contact Brian:

Email: Brian@BrianHiteGlobal.com

www.BrianHiteGlobal.com

www.BeginAgainPerformancePsychology.com

(Bonus Content – Edited Material) – www.BrianHiteGlobal.com/BonusContent

Crystal Shelton

Crystal Shelton, a former Hot Mess Professional immersed in a decade of the corporate world of high stress, embarked on her own transformational journey. Rekindling her passion for art and music, and she reconnected with her higher purpose in guiding others as she practiced loving herself again.

With the onset of her coaching career, Crystal delved into empowering others to reduce stress levels, using Mind Shifting tools to eliminate their anxiety, and SHARING how to create good health, loving their bodies, thrive in their relationships and freaking LOVE their lives!

She discovered a gap in the stress relief industry. To bridge that gap, Crystal pioneered the Zen Mind Mastery System to truly transform stress, anxiety and the continuous chaos of the Hot Mess Professional into resilience, strength, peace, love and tranquility of the Zen Mind Master. Through Soul Fuel, Mind Shifting and Self Mastery you become a Zen Mind Master managing stress even in continuous high-pressure situations and living a Zen life filled with peace, love, and serenity. This leads to improved health, ease, relationships, and positive self-image.

Her impactful work has touched the lives of over a thousand individuals, including friends, clients, and students, in her roles as a Certified Life Coach, Certified Biofield Practitioner, Reiki Master, and Leadership Coach.

Transforming Stress into Serenity

By Crystal Shelton

I WAS A HOT MESS

In the hustle and bustle of our modern world, amidst the overwhelming sea of responsibilities, expectations, and uncertainties, stress seems to be the norm nowadays. Often, finding inner peace can feel like an elusive dream. Yet, in the depths of our being, there exists a sea of ease and flow just waiting to be tapped into—a reservoir of resilience that empowers us to navigate life's storms with grace and fortitude.

When we master regulating the stress in our body, something exciting and unexplainable happens. We feel ALIVE! The mind has an eagle eye focus, the body has more capacity, and our relationships shift to loving and togetherness.

Below, as I share my transformational story with you, I intend to inspire you to create spaciousness and alignment in your own life. Even if we cannot see it, often, the path we are looking for is right in front of us!

My story starts with my great excitement about my wedding. The day of my wedding to the man I love was fast approaching, and, as you can imagine, there was so much to do that I was straining my limits. Before I could leave for my two-week tropical honeymoon, there was so much to do. I remember the several weeks of preparation before my wedding, and my excitement at that time could light a bonfire. At the same time, a deep dread hit me internally.

You see, back then, I was trapped in the corporate world of high stress. My boss was the VP of IT for a large corporation, and she was a relentless force to deal with, often demanding my assistance at all times of the day. Because my job was never-ending, I worked consistently and usually felt unbearable pressure dragging me down. Friends and family voiced concerns about my mental and physical health. I was a *hot mess*. My determination to provide value to the company kept me going. Even with all my efforts I usually felt I was only mildly recognized, and most often ignored completely.

When my boss made it clear that I was not allowed to take two weeks off unless she and her team received seamless support, I closed my office door, broke down, and cried.

Fortunately, one of my colleagues generously offered to cover for me so that I could truly be "OFF WORK" during my honeymoon!

I was so relieved, yet the absolute dread of what she would deal with lingered in my mind. My job was almost too taxing for any one person, let alone someone trying to keep up with two demanding jobs.

I remember asking my colleague about this with great concern. "Are you sure?"

"Oh, yes! You deserve to have an amazing time with your honey on your fabulous Caribbean Honeymoon!" She reassured me with a smile.

"Thank you so much!" I said with tears of gratitude in my eyes. "I don't know how I can ever repay you!"

Even with her reassurance, I couldn't shake the feeling of impending disaster. The workload was immense, and I knew she would be overwhelmed in my absence.

In the weeks before my wedding, I continued to be a hot mess, pushing the stress down into my body, working even more stressful hours, knowing the avalanche of work that was about to hit my temporary substitute. Late nights and early mornings became my norm as I struggled to get ahead of my massive to-do list.

Then, to add to the mix, my mom came to visit. I was hoping to spend some quality time with her before the rapidly approaching BIG DAY. But, instead of taking time off to relax and enjoy her company like I so dearly wanted, I found myself chained to a virtual desk through my laptop, and I was drowning in a sea of emails and deadlines.

Two days before my wedding, I still felt the heavy load, but I cut back to a 6-hour day instead of my normal 10-12 hours just so I could prepare for my wedding. Before I could let go of work, I officially handed everything over to my colleague and logged off my work email. With a guarded sigh of relief, I signed off and shut down my computer.

It was TIME to focus on MY LIFE.

It comes back to me like it was yesterday: "Today is my wedding day! Woohoo!" I exclaimed as I looked in the mirror. Wait, what is that? WTH!! I saw a tiny little cold sore on my top lip. Those nasty little things always showed up when the pressure was too much. This physical manifestation showed me JUST HOW MUCH the stress has been eating at me over the last few weeks and, honestly, for the last couple of years.

As my precious wedding day saw the sun move across the sky, I smiled with relief as the beautiful blue and white lilacs were placed along the path to the lake's edge, where I would soon say my vows with my man.

I let myself relax by playing a song on my guitar. Playing my guitar was my sanctuary, and it always released any stress I was holding onto. It was my *soul fuel*.

By the time I was fixing my hair and getting dressed, holy cow, I realized how fast the stress was turning up the heat! My heart sank as that little demonic cold sore had grown to about the size of a dime! HUGE!!! And ON MY WEDDING DAY!

"What am I going to do?" I panicked.

I covered the monstrous scab the best I could with layers of makeup to hide what had developed on my face.

And then it hit me like a ton of bricks: this wasn't just about a cold sore. It was about the toll that stress was taking on my life—physically, emotionally, and mentally. Yes, the extra 20 pounds were overwhelming. I felt guilty about my daily alcohol consumption used to numb the stress and pain, and I realized the stress was also straining my relationships with my soon-to-be husband and my teenage boys, and it just killed me. But more than that, there was the constant feeling of being trapped, of sacrificing my happiness for the sake of a job that didn't appreciate me.

As the wedding music started to play, I pushed down the embarrassment about my lip. Arm in arm, my handsome sons escorted me down the path to the lake with tears of joy as I saw my soon-to-be husband waiting for me with a big smile on his face. For the moment, everything in my life was amazing and beautiful. All the while, deep inside, underneath the happy and excited exterior, I also felt like a fraud.

This experience was the turning point in my life. I really couldn't continue living like this, letting the stress and work consume me and define who I was. This wake-up call shook me to my core.

I finally told myself…

I am NOT my job.

I am NOT who I work for.

I am NOT who I am married to, although I love him dearly.

I deserve MORE, and it's finally time to start living for myself and creating the life I want!

STRESS UNVEILED

Before I continue with my story, let's delve into the reality of stress and the deep impact it creates on our bodies. Stress is essentially how the mind and body react to events around us, with the body's fight/flight/freeze response. Imagine a deer that runs away when it suspects danger. Once the perceived danger is over, it calmly goes back to grazing. Deer do not worry.

As humans, we experience events and memories from our past, which could be from yesterday or years ago. The mind automatically creates meanings and replays these events as if they are happening now. The body perceives this stress as a current danger and moves energy from processes like digestion and cell repair to our arms and legs to get ready to run or fight even though there really is no current danger!

Consider the continuous stress scenario of a modern professional. You may process 300+ emails, 40 tasks, plus 2-4 hours of meetings every single day for months on end, then go home and take care of the household, the marriage, the kids, soccer mom responsibilities, cleaning the house, cooking dinner, and…must I go on?

If this is resonating, you are probably going nonstop, working out and no matter what you eat you still gain weight, feeling constantly stressed and overwhelmed, indeed a hot mess.

The Chaos Carousel looks like feeling tired constantly for more than a month, snapping at your spouse or kids more than you want, and finding yourself feeling guilty after turning to alcohol or smoking to "relax" after your day, only to repeat it all the next day.

You have most likely heard that when professionals talk about stress relief, they mention self-care and activities like meditation, deep breathing, gratitude, and journaling.

These are all excellent ways to start, but these activities are often a temporary fix at best. If you have ever jumped into your car right after a relaxing massage and someone cuts you off on the freeway, and you snap, immediately screaming at them like a road rage maniac, then you know what I am saying.

Maybe you meditate during your "morning routine" to feel happy and peaceful, only to have some minuscule event throw off your energy and attitude for hours or even days?

The beginner "self-care" strategies above are great starter techniques that bring relief every time we practice them, but the deeper-level tools in my program provide long-lasting results. The primary key to self-care is to practice these tools daily and as often as needed. None of these tools are a do-it-once-and-the-problem-is-gone type of thing.

Stress relief is much like bathing. Do you shower once, and then YAY, you are done? Haha! Nope! We shower every day to stay clean, feel good, and keep our bodies healthy. Self-care is the same. It is necessary to practice self-care every day and in more than one way to sustain the results of peace and joy.

But stress affects more than our mental state—it takes a toll on our physical health as well. Chronic stress can weaken the immune system, making us more susceptible to illness. It can lead to weight gain, high blood pressure, and even contribute to heart disease. The constant release of the stress hormone Cortisol can disrupt sleep patterns, leaving us fatigued and irritable.

The steady stream of stress can also wreak havoc on our relationships. I realize you know this already, but it bears repeating that when stressed, we are more likely to snap at loved ones before thinking about it, leading to arguments and even deeply held resentments.

This strain on relationships only adds to our overall stress levels, creating a vicious cycle of tension and conflict. In short, stress is a silent killer, slowly chipping away at our health, happiness, and well-being. If you pardon the pun, I would like to stress that it is essential to take proactive steps to manage stress and prioritize your self-care, not just for our own sake but also, and maybe just as important, for the sake of those we love.

MY TRANSFORMATIONAL SHIFT

It was the moment I needed to go back to loving myself, but I did not know what to do or where to start. Out of the blue, a friend invited me to a "Women's Event" in San Diego. I had no idea what to expect. Honestly, I was terrified! My heart beat frantically, hoping

I could hide the chaos manifesting inside me. I wanted so badly to leave early, to sail away without being noticed!

The first two days, I tried to 'hide in plain sight' as the speaker, a beautiful, confident, and powerful woman, presented all these empowering new ideas and concepts. I was absolutely sure that she could only see the smile on my face and not the damage I had subconsciously processed and integrated into my life.

I was wrong...

On the 3rd day, everything changed. I released my fear and cried - A LOT.

I met the woman who soon became my coach. She guided me down a path of joy and peace that I didn't even realize was directly right in front of me. My whole life shifted when I felt the world lift from my shoulders as I FINALLY realized...there *was another way*.

Could I truly have WHAT I REALLY WANTED?

Could I really truly be happy?

Could I have a beautiful marriage, a sexy and healthy body, and an amazing job or business?

Could I not only expect all these things but feel like I deserve them?

The Answer was YES! (and it still is!)

Suddenly, HOPE had returned to me. Hope that seemed to avoid me at all costs in the past.

The hot mess Crystal, toiling through the mountains of stress, slowly became a distant memory. I connected with my personal power, the magic of saying NO, and strengthened my emotional and energetic boundaries.

I spent years of self-introspection, reading, manifesting, emotional and physical healing, and a strong focus on leadership with my coach. I found exactly where normal "stress-relief" guidance was lacking. Please don't be discouraged, but the guidance I found on the internet and in books seemed so superficial and unrealistic. I remember asking myself, "How can I simply think my way to gratitude? And who can actually sit quietly and meditate for 30 minutes?" I laughed because I couldn't sit still quietly and do nothing for 5 minutes without feeling guilty and thinking I should be doing something! Then, I wondered who in the world has TIME for all of the activities outlined in these books.

But I tried anyway. I tried to do what they said, only to find this huge gap. As my frustration grew, I discovered many mistakes embedded in the self-care advice that I had found.

Being a Hot Mess Professional (ha-ha), this cycle kept happening because I was constantly doing 10+ things at once and never actually finishing them. I didn't feel like I had TIME to do things for myself, and you might feel the same way. For example, "Self-Care" is selfish and highly overrated.

To fix this, I bet you have tried working harder to finally make a dent in that to-do list, only to find yourself working harder to no avail. You may have even tried going to bed early only to stay awake worrying about what tomorrow will bring, and maybe even tried and failed at some of the "self-care" tools everyone talks about, only to find yourself still tired, still spinning like a top and wondering when the chaos carousel is going to stop and let you off.

YOUR FIRST SIMPLE STEP:

What is an activity that you LOVE to do and could literally do this all day?

What activity gives you energy?

This is your Soul Fuel.

Integrating your Soul Fuel into your daily life will quickly transform how you feel about yourself every day and how you respond to others around you. The key is consistency. Finding within yourself the fortitude to continue with what you practice even when things are busy and especially when things are going really well. This will also create profound changes in your attitude, but you will have to experience it firsthand to really believe it! I promise the transformation you will feel from this first step will shift your life, but just imagine what the next level of mastery over your words and behavior can do to improve your life!

Let me provide you with a couple of examples.

#1:

One anxious client said his Soul Fuel was working out. It had been years since he had worked out consistently! He was resistant when I asked him to commit to working out and living his crazy busy life. Once he created a consistent exercise program, using the Mind Shifting tools to manage his language, mind, attitude, and behavior, he found anxiety was a distant memory, his job became easier, and he had more energy for his friends and hobbies after work!

#2:

A student I worked with said coaching others was her Soul Fuel. However, her mindset was resentful that she was giving all of her energy and time away helping others. The Mind Shifting tools switched her mindset, and the coaching actually filled her soul instead of the activity draining her. Her whole life was transformed, creating ease and flow in every crack and crevice!

Hopefully, these examples will give you an idea that once you recognize your Soul Fuel and consistently DO it, you will start to see the transformation you seek.

CONTINUED LEARNING

I once had a new client ask me, "How long is this going to take for me to learn?"

My answer was, "You can learn the Zen Mind Mastery tools in just a couple of months. It's practice that takes the time and that all depends on you. The more you fully immerse yourself in the practice, the more effective it will be in your life and the longer the changes will last."

Want to know a secret? Every action you take in every moment is either beneficial or not. :)

Be on the lookout for books by me, about unleashing your greatness, stepping into ease and flow and living the life you have always envisioned. I love supporting and connecting with new people. My impactful work has touched the lives of over a thousand individuals, including friends, clients, and students, in my roles as a Certified Life Coach, Certified Biofield Tuning Practitioner, Reiki Master, and Leadership Coach.

***

To Contact Crystal:

Email: Crystal@RealLifeVisions.com

Website: www.reallifevisions.com

LinkedIn: https://www.linkedin.com/in/crystal-shelton-2aa2b420/

Facebook: https://www.facebook.com/crystal.shelton.1485

Instagram: https://www.instagram.com/reallifevisionsstresscoach/

Charla Anderson

Joy is my lifestyle. Unconditional Love is my message. Mindset is my method. Mom. Nana. 34-year award-winning flight attendant, retired. Olympic Torch bearer. Your Inspired Speaker. Your Courageous Coach. Author of 2 best-selling books, 'Candy Bar Hugs~It Doesn't Take Much to Make a Difference' 'Split-Second Transformation~Change Your Words, Change Your Life: 31 Daily Practices'. Host of the TV show and podcast, 'The Charla Anderson Show~Collector & Connector of Fascinating People (& Everyone is Fascinating!)' on WinWinWomen.tv. Ziglar Legacy Certified Trainer. Engaging Podcast Guest. Outrageously Optimistic. Outrageously Courageous. Personal Development Junkie. I've earned every single one of these silver hairs the hard way and have a plethora of life experiences to share. ('Charla' is a derivative of 'chat' in Spanish, and 'Joy' in Greek. My parents were prophets and didn't know it, lol). I have proudly entered my 7th decade, and I ain't slowin' down! OH, and I am shamelessly happy to live in the Fort Worth, Texas area! 🐵

My favorite Sayings:

'When Intriguing opportunities present themselves, and you say YES, things show up';

'Unconditional Love. Unconditional Forgiveness. NOT unconditional boundaries.'

'You can't change THE world, but you can change YOUR world, which changes THE WORLD!'

'Everything is always working out for me!'

Unleashing Potential:
A Journey of Transformation and Empowerment
By Charla Anderson

Is a life lived in one paragraph? How do you fill in the spaces between those words? The ups, downs, ins, outs, joys, sorrows, struggles, heartbreaks, tragedies, life, death, stillborn, births, first steps, proud moments, love, kisses, hugs, friends, challenges, takeoffs and touchdowns, layovers, mission trips, neighborhood house with the pool, Scouts, six-grade squeaky band concerts... and does anyone even care about YOUR dash? Or mine 1953-?

An optimist even in high school, I remember saying, "I'm high on life! I don't need drugs and stuff..." Therefore, thankfully, I was never even offered them... Even back then, I seemed to know that attitude was important, and that words really matter. Now, as I continue to study mindset and the miraculous law of attraction, my message that *every word matters* is even more relevant in our current world today.

When you embark on a career that ultimately spans 34 years, it truly becomes your identity. At 20 years old, landing the dream job of being a flight attendant, I was assigned my base in the frozen city of Chicago. After being raised in Houston, Texas (yes, I had seen snow a couple of times, on Valentine's Day in kindergarten and college), my first purchase was a sheepskin coat. I still have it. Those northerners asked me about my oil wells and horses, and I asked them about the mafia and bank robbers. Movies and perception turn out to be as real as you allow them to be! As it turned out, my year of living in Chicago was wonderfully fun, young and dynamic time.

Moving back to Houston, I got married, had kids, got divorced, moved to the DFW area, re-married, divorced again and it all happened so fast. 'Who I AM' was a flight attendant and a mom. I literally expected to be the oldest living flight attendant still serving in my 80's+. I loved my job. My passengers were my mission field. Being peer nominated, then selected to carry the Olympic Torch for the Salt Lake City Olympics, was my highest honor, as well as being a recipient of the Chairman's Club award, allows me to say that I was an award-winning flight attendant. Somehow, one day they offered a retirement package in 2008, and I took it… and cried for the last three months of my beautiful career. *Oh, the places we would go; the people we would meet; the miles we would walk at 35 thousand feet.*

Exiting that wonderful world in the airline industry, I was frankly lost. With my kids grown and my beloved job behind me, it was interesting to learn that there was a world of networking. *I had no idea* that the networking world existed. Chambers and leads groups, and meet-ups, etc. Since I had sold Mary Kay, and love my Zurvita network marketing company, I quickly began collecting business cards, realizing a little too late that those networking groups did not look fondly on the MLM industry. Regardless, I captured baskets full of business cards, with no idea what to do with them. I had no real understanding of the nuances of the business connection world. I met incredibly wonderful people, and loved encouraging everyone… I just never made any money. Since I am NOT money motivated, I kept going, *because I love people.* Many of those original connections are still good friends to this day.

One day, as I was enjoying a meal at a restaurant, a buzz started when a man walked in, "He has his own radio show!" I was introduced, invited to the studio he was airing his show from, and within a week had my own show! That was in 2013. WOW! Now I AM a radio show host! Imagine a live 2-hour weekly talk show from a beautiful studio… well, I know how to talk. My name is a derivative of 'chat' in Spanish, (and 'Joy' in Greek), so why not? After a few solo shows, I began hosting guests. I met some amazing people along the way, including many from my connection with the Ziglar family. Oh, yes, I had met so many wonderful people (including Zig) at the Monday morning weekly devotionals that are ongoing to this day. After a year or so, I changed studios, and because I never monetized it, chose to give up my show after 3 wonderful years. When Tom, Julie and Cindy Ziglar began a program to memorialize their Dad's incredible life, I was honored to become one of the first 95 members of Ziglar Legacy Certified Trainers, my most treasured credential, in November of 2014.

Shifting back to some of the spaces between the words of that first paragraph, I loved living in the cutest little house for five years. Rent was increasing. In 2017, my dear friend Carlene called and convinced me that it was time for a change, that she wanted me to come to East Texas and help her build a retreat center. So, I packed up my little house, and took out on a 6-week trek (already planned) living *from* my car (not *in* it). Most of my stuff got put into storage upstairs in my ex-husband's house. I had given him the house that we raised our kids in when we divorced, and since he had bad knees, he wasn't using the stairs often anyway.

The first month was just a wonderful time house-sitting for Joyce and Wayne, my sister and brother-in-law in the Hill Country of Texas, watching the dog, ducks, donkey, chickens, goats, pond and pool. It was so nice. I had been working on my first book and coaching program, and in that peaceful environment was able to finish writing my tiny book with a BIG message, "Candy Bar Hugs~It Doesn't Take Much to Make a Difference!" (a pay-it-forward book with stories about offering a candy bar and a hug to check-out cashiers). While there, I also named my coaching program CAP: Courage, Authority, Peace/Prosperity. I called it 'Charla's Outrageously Courageous Life Mentoring System'. Was it prophetic? What do you think?

After that first month, there was an already scheduled Zurvita event the next weekend in Memphis, TN. As I left my little paradise, I claimed (as I always do) God's shield of protection. Psalm 91 has every protection promise in one chapter, and I claim and proclaim it often. "Thank You" is my mantra. *Thank You* for your umbrella of protection. *Thank You* for protecting my car, my home, my children, my family.... *Thank YOU* is always running through my head. Gratitude is the key to a satisfied life.

As I was finding my way to the Airbnb I would be sharing with my friend, I made a necessary stop. The gas station had no working bathroom. The one across the street did, but no door or tp. I was witness to some very sad situations, where respect and dignity were absent, and it seemed that the 'system' had sold out this lovely town.

After a big happy networking convention event on Saturday night, my friend Chri and I were walking up the driveway of the Airbnb. Suddenly, the two bags in my right hand (with all my favorite convention clothes, cowboy boots, new MacBook, makeup, etc.) were ripped from my hand. My Yeti flung to the ground, and I found a gun at my head. Chri had already handed her backpack to one of the young men. My left hand was clinging to my purse, and the young man was grabbing at it, saying, "Give me your purse. Give me your keys!"

HERE IS THE STORY: I literally stepped towards the gun that was at held at my temple, and said, "Y'all need LOVE!" They ran. What is most surprising to most people is that I had ZERO fear. Of course, I was shaken, but not afraid. WHY? Because WHO I AM, is who I have said that I AM for many years. WHO I AM is "Bold Faith, NO fear!" I do not remember when I started claiming it, but in the moment of TRUTH, it was my truth. Earlier I said that *every word matters*! Those two young men thought that these two old ladies would be easy targets. (I say, 'Don't Mess with Texas!' lol). In that moment, I knew that I would win either way. Either meet Jesus, or keep my purse, keys and *phone* (remember, I was living FROM my car, so it could have been a much more difficult situation had they taken them). My Angels were all around me, as my shield of protection, and I knew it.

SO, who I say that I AM is Bold Faith, NO fear. Remember what I named my coaching program just a week before the robbery? Charla's Outrageously Courageous Life Mentoring System. Can I claim that I AM Outrageously Courageous? Can I claim that I AM Bold Faith, NO fear? I find it quite fascinating, in so many ways.

They did actually shoot the gun as they were leaving. The police found the 9mm shell. For more about this story, look for my forthcoming book "*Outrageously Courageous~Bold Faith, NO fear: Step Towards the Gun!*"

Because I AM who I SAY THAT I AM, I Get to Choose! I AM Bold Faith, NO fear. I AM Outrageously Courageous. I AM Outrageously Optimistic. I AM Hugs. I AM Joy. I AM Peace. I AM Light. I AM unconditional LOVE.

When you say "I Am..." you are defining YOU. 'I AM' is proclaiming and naming YOU. Every. Word. Matters! Speak only what you want, who you want to be, where you want to go. You get more of what you think about, so why not think positively? You become who you say that you are, so why not claim good things?

My identity is no longer tied to my career. Or my family. Or my associations. It never has been about my possessions. My identity is my character. My acts of service. My integrity. My love for humanity. I loved being a flight attendant. I love being Mom and Nana. AND I was all of those other values all along.

Consider your values. Deeply. Is your time and your money spent on what you say is important to you? A good values barometer is monitoring your calendar and bank account… do they indicate that perhaps you value entertainment more than family time, for instance? Just asking… Bold boundaries around your core values are worth evaluating often. My 'Adults Need Boundaries Too' workshop featuring the *Boundaries Barometer*™ offers guidance for you through this thought-intensive conversation towards building your Legacy message.

Another story in that dash is that after staying with another sister, Marsha, in Tennessee for a couple of weeks, I headed back towards East Texas. It turns out that the girl I was going to rent a room from backed out while I was in route. So it turned out that I moved back into the house with my ex-husband Edd, upstairs.

In those chaotic times amid boxes and messes, I somehow got my book self-published, I started my own TV show, was directly involved with *America's Real Deal* TV show's first episode in the wonderful Stockyards of Fort Worth, and traveled to multiple patriotic events around the country, meeting many influential people. A year or so later Edd moved to be with his family, and I began working toward updating the 25-year-old house.

Well... Then came the kids, circling back with their animals, stuff, kids, friends, messes, etc. I love them, *and* it feels good to have peace and quiet again. Having my grand blissing live with me the first two years of her life was the absolute delight of my life. I have an album called 'Sarissa's first year in Nana's lap' with hundreds of sweet pictures. And, finally, at this moment in 2024, I am reclaiming my home, as I write this chapter. Here's to another new season.

Because I have been living upstairs all these years, and because I now have an empty master suite with a separate back entrance, I am embarking on a new venture of landlord, turning the bedroom into a lovely rental for airline commuters, traveling nurses or corporate travelers; a safe and convenient place for someone's home-away-from-home. It is being updated and readied right now, and is comfortable, cozy, warm and welcoming. I've named it 'Shirley's Sweet Suite', after my beautiful late sister Shirley Hooks. It pays to have my very dear friend, Patricia, who can literally do anything, with an eye for detail and excellence, take my projects on as if they were hers. A tireless miracle worker (and makes me do hard work too!). It would be a mediocre space without her expertise and commitment to blessing me. Priceless.

The first week of January each year for the past 4 years, I have taken a week away, to a quiet cottage to recharge and regroup. One of my favorite sayings is, "when intriguing opportunities present themselves, and you say YES, things show up!" And they do. I answered an email with a call and ended up with my own weekly live television show in 2023, *"The Charla Anderson Show~Collector & Connector of Fascinating People (and Everyone is Fascinating!)"* on the WinWin Women network, now in season 2, and on podcasts, and going strong. There is no lack of fascinating people with incredible stories of overcoming, offering hope and wit and wisdom, and I love having conversations and sharing them with the world. Once again back in the media world, which is quite ironic to me since I so rarely watch TV.

As I have now entered my 7th decade on this remarkable planet, it feels great to continue learning, growing, giving and expanding my horizons… I won't stop hugging, or sending love and blessings, or encouraging you to be your best self by *watching your words*, and your manners, and your values. My book, *"Split-Second Transformation~Change Your Words, Change Your Life: 31 Daily Practices"*, completed during the chaos of these last few years, and launched last year on my 70th birthday, November 30th, offers daily reminders and encouragement to manifest what is important to you by speaking only what you want.

What's next? One of the blessings of my life is the people that I am surrounded with. One of my long-time declarations is, "I attract successful people willing to invest in me", which has continually manifested with some amazing people in my life, including those involved with '*The Change*' Book Series. This is a labor of love by Jim Britt, Jim Lutes, and every author I have met. Their commitment to the success of every one of us is beyond refreshing along with the very high-level mentoring we receive. This book is a level-up steppingstone for my exciting future of speaking, workshops, events, writing and coaching. Many new very talented friends are willing to partner with me as I step into my Queen energy, step into my purpose of radiating Light and Love into the world and raising the vibration of the universe.

I'm not slowing down… and I ain't quittin'! I invite you to continue the conversation with me and join me in my *Legacy Builder Society* membership. Let's keep in touch. Smiles and Hugs!

***

To contact Charla:

Charla@CharlaAnderson.com

CharlaAnderson.com

Charla@CharlaAnderson.com

Facebook.com/CharlaArnold

Facebook.com/CandyBarHugs

Facebook.com/TheCharlaAShow

LinkedIn.com/CharlaA

YouTube.com/@CharlaAndersonShow

Jerry Roisentul

Jerry Roisentul is an entrepreneurial force and a visionary in network marketing and business with over 30 years of experience. His expertise in mindset management, leadership, and team building, honed through personal challenges and triumphs, has made him a sought-after mentor and speaker. Over the last decade, Jerry has traveled worldwide, training thousands of people to identify and eliminate the mindset obstacles that limit their potential and to obtain their Champion Mindsets.

Jerry knows from firsthand experience that the difference between success and struggle is almost always an issue of mindset. In 2006, after suffering devastating loss on every side, he fell into a thick depression in which he intended to take his own life. Thankfully, he survived that dark time and spent the next five years of his life on a journey of self-discovery and introspection that caused him to understand one crucial thing--mindset was the most powerful tool he had. Having experienced deep pain and hardship, Jerry can channel that empathy into connecting with audiences at the soul level.

He is a Certified Coach, Speaker, and Trainer with The Maxwell Leadership Team, the author of the best-selling and award-winning book, "Don't Let Doubt Take You Out," and was recently recognized as one of the distinguished Top 10 Iconic 100 Impact Ignitors of 2023 in the category of Leadership & Mindset Development.

His captivating and passionate presentations and trainings will help propel you to success to achieve all you've been created to be.

Transforming Failures into Victory: My Journey of Overcoming Doubt and Fear and Cultivating a Resilient Mindset.

By Jerry Roisentul

Once upon a time, in the tumultuous realm of elementary school, there lived a brave adventurer named... Well, let's just call him "Me." And so, our tale begins at the tender age of 9, when the world was a playground, and crushes were as common as recess.

Enter Stephanie – the dazzling beauty of our school, with a smile that could outshine the sun and a laugh that could make even the grumpiest lunch lady crack a smile. Ah yes, Stephanie, the object of my youthful affection, the muse of my daydreams, and the cause of more butterflies in my stomach than a colony of monarchs migrating south for the winter.

Now, picture this: the winter dance was fast approaching, casting its spell of jittery nerves upon the halls of our school. And there I was, a pint-sized Casanova in the making (at least in my own mind), determined to summon the courage to ask Stephanie if she would do me the honor of accompanying me to the dance.

But courage proved to be as elusive as a snowflake in June. Every time I found myself in Stephanie's presence, my tongue tied itself into knots, my palms grew sweatier than a snowman in a sauna, and all coherent thought abandoned ship faster than you can say, "frozen yogurt."

And oh, my friends – those mischievous rascals who took great delight in reminding me of all the reasons why Stephanie would sooner sprout wings and fly to the moon than accept my humble invitation. With each whispered doubt and raised eyebrow, my confidence dwindled, melting away under the harsh glare of their skepticism.

Now, here's the twist: the doubts that loomed in my mind were nothing more than whispers of insecurity, echoes of fear that threatened to drown out the beating of my brave little heart. In my quest to shield myself from rejection, I unwittingly built up a fortress of regret – a monument to the dance that could have been if only I had dared to dream a little bigger.

Little did I realize at that moment that the doubts and fears I encountered would wield a profound influence on the trajectory of my life ahead.

My journey in overcoming doubt and fear and transforming my mindset has been a rollercoaster ride filled with valuable lessons and significant growth. I hope that as I share some of the things I've learned along the way in this chapter, it can help make a difference in your life as well.

Like many entrepreneurial professionals, I have faced countless moments of self-doubt and fear throughout my career. There were times when I questioned my abilities and felt overwhelmed by the challenges ahead. But instead of letting these negative emotions consume me, I consciously confronted them head-on and learned how to master my mindset instead of my mindset mastering me.

One pivotal moment in my journey was realizing that doubt and fear are natural parts of the process. They are not indicators of failure or incompetence but steppingstones towards growth and success. I started viewing doubt as an opportunity to learn and improve and fear as a sign that I was pushing myself out of my comfort zone.

To conquer doubt, I began focusing on my strengths and achievements. I started by making a list of my accomplishments, big and small, to remind myself of the progress I had already made. I sought feedback from trusted mentors and peers, allowing their perspectives to neutralize my doubts.

I also surrounded myself with a supportive network of like-minded individuals who understood my struggles. I gained camaraderie and encouragement by building relationships with people who shared similar goals and aspirations. Together, we formed a support system that propelled us forward when doubt and fear threatened to hold us back. This also helped me realize an important fact of life: never take advice from anyone more messed up than you.

Transforming my mindset required a conscious effort to reframe negative thoughts and beliefs. I practiced positive affirmations and visualizations, consistently reminding myself of my capabilities and potential. I sought motivational resources like books, podcasts, and seminars to fuel my inspiration and maintain a positive mindset.

Additionally, I recognized the importance of taking calculated risks. I understood that growth lies outside my comfort zone, and I needed to embrace uncertainty and the possibility of failure. I gradually built resilience and confidence by pushing myself to step into uncomfortable situations and confront my fears.

Ultimately, my journey in overcoming doubt and fear and transforming my mindset is ongoing. By adopting a positive and proactive approach, I have experienced tremendous growth and achieved milestones I once deemed impossible.

Let me share with you two very vulnerable, authentic, and transparent stories of how I overcame doubt in some of the most challenging endeavors in my life.

In 2006, I experienced one of the darkest times of my life. I was going through a divorce with my son's mom after ten years of marriage and having built a successful network marketing business together; I was in a deep state of depression as I went from seeing my son (who was three years old at the time) every day to only on the weekends. The business his mom and I built together began to implode in front of my eyes. All of that led me to the floor of my apartment on a cold night in November of 2006.

Beside me lay a bottle of pills, a grim testament to my intentions. I took out a notepad and a pen and started writing a letter.

"My dearest son, I love you more than anything in the world and I want you to know that you are the greatest thing that has ever happened to me. Sometimes, life gets difficult and challenging, so I am writing you this letter to try my best to explain to you, when you get older, why your dad took his own life."

As I got through those first few sentences, I went into a rage: I hurled objects, shattered fragile remnants of my former life, screamed at the top of my lungs, and pounded the floor with unrestrained fury. How could this be happening to me?

I was the motivator, the encourager, and the guy everyone went to for inspiration, guidance, and direction. How could **THAT** guy have ended up on the floor getting ready to end it all?

Back then, my relationship with God was distant at best. Yet, today, He is the center of my life. I am convinced, with unwavering conviction, that God intervened that fateful night, preserving my life for a purpose far beyond my comprehension at the time. That is why Jeremiah 29:11 has become my life scripture: **"I know the plans I have for you," says the LORD, "Plans to prosper you and not harm you; to give you a hope and a future."**

In the ensuing weeks, a profound realization came upon me, one that would leave an indelible mark on my future: During times of triumph, when achievements flowed effortlessly, and success seemed so simple, I was managing my mindset. Yet, when plunged into despair, with hope slipping through my fingers, it was my mindset that began managing me.

It was at that point I understood that we cannot always control the events and situations that happen in our lives, but we have **TOTAL CONTROL** over how we react and respond to them.

The resilience I exhibited during that pivotal moment in my life propelled me to establish my coaching and mentoring business, Champion Mentorship, Inc., six years later in 2012. Through this venture, I've had the opportunity to journey across the globe, utilizing the insights and lessons from my personal struggles to help leaders break through the obstacles hindering them from fulfilling their potential and purpose. Witnessing people's lives undergo positive transformation, and observing the breaking of chains that once hindered them is among the most fulfilling experiences in my life, stemming from the lessons gleaned from my adversities.

My second story takes place in 2011, right before I started my company. I faced a daunting challenge when a friend asked me to do a training session for her team at her leadership meeting. Despite my lack of experience in coaching, my friend suggested I offer a 45-minute coaching session to the 30 individuals in attendance for just $20. Initially, I was confused, thinking, "Who would want to coach with me after meeting me for just 45 minutes?" However, to my surprise, 15 people accepted the offer. Panic set in as I realized I had no training materials, no courses, events, or direction. Quite honestly, I had no clue.

To cope with the overwhelming doubt, I began to feel; I personified it by giving it a name – Dan Doubt. (You can also call it Debbie Doubt if you'd like, but this just worked for me.) He became a regular character in the story of my life. He followed me everywhere I went, looking for an opportunity to tear me down. Whenever you hear those voices in your mind telling you that you can't, you won't, you shouldn't, what do you know about this topic? You're broke; you've failed at everything you've tried. You know the voices I am talking about? If you do, then congratulations on already having met Dan Doubt in your own life.

With my first coaching session on the horizon, I desperately needed to rush through it before my clients realized I had no idea what I was doing. That first client not only signed up for a six-month coaching program but also brought in several more clients. This sudden success amplified my doubt as I questioned how I would sustain such momentum for six whole months. Dan Doubt reveled in this uncertainty, bombarding me with thoughts of failure, embarrassment, and destroying my reputation.

However, the story did not end there. Out of the first ten people I coached with my special $20 session, eight of them signed up for extended coaching. Overwhelmed and feeling over my head, I turned to the strategies I had learned and applied throughout my journey. By managing my doubt, acting despite my fear, and continuously implementing the tools outlined in my bestselling book, "Don't Let Doubt Take You Out," I could overcome the doubts I faced every day.

Throughout my journey, one principle I've steadfastly believed in is the importance of furnishing an Action List following any valuable teaching or sharing. This list comprises tangible steps individuals can take to effectively utilize the acquired knowledge.

Along the path of my personal growth, I've realized this profound truth: Inspiration **WITHOUT** Application will keep you in Frustration, relegating us to the status of professional students. While we accumulate knowledge, its true impact remains dormant without practical implementation.

However, Inspiration **WITH** Application creates Transformation. This is where the magic happens, a catalyst for profound change in our lives.

I want to provide you with an Action Steps Checklist to summarize all that we covered and give you an easy way to decide which ones you are doing well and which you may need to work on personally and professionally.

Action Steps Checklist:

1. Cultivate a Growth Mindset:

- Encourage yourself to adopt a growth mindset by believing in your ability to develop through dedication and hard work.

- View failures and setbacks as opportunities for growth and learning.

- Emphasize the importance of perseverance in the face of challenges. Never, ever give up.

2. Embrace Collaboration and Networking:

- Actively seek opportunities for collaboration and networking.

- Attend industry conferences, join professional associations, and engage in online communities.

- Highlight the benefits of expanding knowledge, connections, and resources through collaboration

3. Set SMART Goals:

- Set Specific, Measurable, Attainable, Relevant, and Time-bound goals.

- Break down your goals into smaller, actionable steps.

- Have a periodic reassessment and adjustment of your goals as needed.

4. Cultivate a Supportive Environment:

- Remember the importance of surrounding yourselves with positive and supportive individuals.

- Seek out mentors, accountability partners, and mastermind groups.

- Always be open to the value of guidance, motivation, and constructive feedback.

5. **Embrace Failure as Feedback:**

- Shift your perspective on failure by highlighting it as an opportunity to learn and grow.

- Reflect on your experiences, identify lessons learned, and make necessary adjustments.

- Remind yourself that successful entrepreneurs have also faced failures and used them to their advantage, and so can you.

6. **Develop Resilience:**

- It's essential for you to develop resilience in the face of obstacles and setbacks.

- Always see challenges as temporary roadblocks rather than insurmountable barriers.

- Practice mindfulness, self-care, and gratitude to build emotional and mental resilience.

7. **Celebrate Small Wins:**

- Celebrate your progress and recognize smaller milestones. The more you celebrate the progress and little victories, the more success you will have.

- Create the momentum, motivation, and sense of accomplishment that small wins provide.

- Boost your confidence to tackle more considerable challenges.

There's something I'd like to point out: I have many friends who are passionate about running marathons—about 25 miles or so. Meanwhile, I struggle to run from my house to my mailbox and back before feeling the need for a nap.

One thing my friends always mention is that during marathons, there are mile markers every 5 miles. These markers not only indicate how far you've come and how much farther you have to go but also serve as moments to celebrate small victories. I believe they're placed there not just for navigation but to combat doubts that may creep into your mind, reminding you of all the reasons you might not finish the race. By celebrating these small wins on the journey to achieving bigger goals, we can keep doubt at bay.

8. Practice Visualization and Affirmations:

- Invest time visualizing the success you want to have.

- Create affirmations that inspire you and speak those over yourself daily. Death and Life are in the power of your tongue, so choose Life.

One point I want to mention about affirmations. I hear from people all the time that their affirmations don't work. What I usually tell them is it's not that they don't work; it's that we usually don't work them correctly.

Merely skimming through affirmations to mark them off your daily to-do list won't cut it. To truly harness their power, you need to infuse every recital with genuine feeling and emotion. Don't merely speak the words; immerse yourself in them. Envision each affirmation vividly: Picture yourself embodying better health, enjoying a lifestyle enriched by the abundance of time, money, and freedom in your life. Whatever you declare, let it resonate within you. Don't just say the words; **FEEL THEM**. The difference it makes is profound.

I wholeheartedly believe in you and the vast potential that resides within you. You have the power to achieve remarkable things and make a positive impact in this world.

My hope and prayer are that my words and experiences can serve as a catalyst for you to unlock your true potential and live a life of purpose and fulfillment.

As we journey towards our goals, we must be wary of the naysayers who may try to discourage us. Do not let their negative voices deter you from pursuing your dreams. Remember, their skepticism does not reflect your abilities but rather a projection of their own fears and insecurities. Stay focused on your vision and surround yourself with those who uplift and inspire you.

Let your life be a shining beacon of hope and inspiration to others. We are all interconnected, and our actions, however small, can create a ripple effect of positive change. Embrace kindness, compassion, and empathy, and watch as your light illuminates the darkness around you.

There will undoubtedly be moments during your journey when the road gets tough and challenges seem insurmountable. I urge you to never give up on yourself or your dreams in those moments. Believe in your abilities, persist with unwavering determination, and trust that success is near. Remember, the most remarkable achievements often arise from the most challenging circumstances.

The most important thing I could encourage you to do now is **TAKE ACTION!** Implement the information in this chapter with unwavering determination. Start small, but start now. Formulate your daily affirmations, visualize your success, practice gratitude, and surround yourself with a community of like-minded individuals who will lift you up on your entrepreneurial journey.

Lastly, I eagerly anticipate the day we can connect in person. The opportunity to connect with you, hear your stories, and witness the positive impact my words have had on your lives would be an absolute honor. Until then, let us continue to inspire and uplift one another from afar.

In closing, I want you to know that you have the power to transform your life and the lives of those around you. Embrace this journey with an open heart, unwavering determination, and unshakeable faith in your abilities. Persist, overcome, and keep pushing forward because the potential for extraordinary greatness lies within you.

It's time to let your light shine brightly for all to see!

With utmost encouragement and unwavering belief,

Coach Jerry.

***

To contact Jerry:

Regarding Keynote Speaking for upcoming conferences or retreats, executive one-on-one coaching sessions or the opportunity for tailored training sessions focused on leadership, mindset, or communication for your business or teams, please don't hesitate to reach out using the contact information below:

Website: www.championmentorship.com

Email: jerry@championmentorship.com

LinkedIN: www.linkedin.com/in/jerryroisentul

Facebook: www.facebook.com/jerryroisentul

Instagram: www.instagram.com/jerryroisentul

Karen Butler

Karen Butler, owner of KBFIT, is a renowned fitness expert dedicated to empowering individuals to achieve their best selves through efficient, effective, optimal fitness. With over 30 years of experience in the fitness industry, Karen has trained in various esteemed establishments, witnessing the common challenges faced by individuals striving for optimal health and fitness. Motivated by her own journey of transformation and the desire to revolutionize outdated training models, Karen developed the KBFIT Training Protocol.

Born in Southern California, Karen's passion for health and fitness was sparked early on as she observed the lack of emphasis on wellness in the mature population. Her personal experiences, including overcoming post-pregnancy weight gain, have fueled her commitment to developing a fitness program that delivers the best results in the least amount of time.

Karen's innovative approach focuses on mastering mindset, managing food intake, and implementing efficient training strategies to optimize physical and mental well-being. With a philosophy centered on simplicity, effectiveness, and sustainability, Karen's mission is to equip individuals to reclaim their time, reshape their bodies, and unlock their true potential.

Through her transformative journey, Karen empowers clients to embrace a new narrative, redefine their relationship with fitness and food, and ultimately lead healthier, more fulfilling lives. Join Karen on the path to unleashing your best self and experience the magic of efficient fitness training that transcends traditional approaches.

The Magic of KBFIT:
Change Your Mind – Change Your Body – Change Your Life.

By Karen Butler

If you are anything like me, and I suspect that most of you are, you want to feel your best, look your best, and perform at your best. My journey into developing a program to optimize health and fitness was born out of over 30 years in the fitness industry, during which I have had the privilege of training in world-class resorts, spas, educational programs, schools and churches, corporate fitness programs, and gyms all over the country. Throughout these experiences, I've witnessed countless individuals wasting their time, working harder and harder, yet achieving fewer and fewer results with outdated training models. I found myself doing the same. I spent countless hours at the gym, training clients, instructing classes, as well as doing my own training. If someone would've told me then what I know now, I would not have believed it was possible to ***train far less while getting far better results.*** My motive and passion were born out of a desire to change all that and to empower individuals to ***get fit once and stay fit*** for the rest of their lives in the most effective and efficient way possible. I embarked on a journey to do just that. After all, I think we can all agree, **HEALTH IS OUR GREATEST WEALTH.**

We live in a fast-paced world; time is a precious commodity, and we all find ourselves struggling to balance the demands of work, family, and personal aspirations. As a co-author of this personal empowerment book, we are on a shared journey to inspire and uplift others, providing them with the tools they need to lead their optimal lives. My chapter is dedicated to sharing my passion, purpose, and expertise in revolutionizing the way we approach health and fitness. Nothing gets me more inspired than to empower individuals with the tools they need to take control of their mind and body. That was the impetus that drove me to develop my training model, **KBFIT.** If you want to learn more right now, you're welcome to visit *KBFIT2020.COM.*

Life is a journey, and my journey is not unlike yours. It has been shaped by my personal experiences, as has yours. With four wonderful sons, who are the loves and lights of my life and my greatest honor, I have firsthand knowledge of the challenges that come with each successive pregnancy. With each birth, I gained more weight. Trust me, the 65 pounds I gained during my fourth pregnancy didn't miraculously disappear when I delivered my 9-pound baby boy. Believe it or not, I was working as a fitness trainer at La Costa Spa in Carlsbad, CA, up until I was seven months pregnant. Clearly, hormones play a crucial role in weight gain, and it seemed like no matter what, my body insisted on storing body fat. So, I absolutely sympathize and relate to those feelings of watching your body morph into a different version of yourself and feeling helpless to change it.

Being fit in your 20's is effortless. In your 30s, you begin to see some changes. By the time you are in your 40s, those changes escalate. In your 50s and 60s, with the hormonal changes that happen to both men and women, you don't even recognize the person staring back at you in the mirror. Your former body is just a memory you only see in photos. These personal experiences have fueled my passion and determination to develop a fitness program that works for real people – people like you and me, to get **THE BEST RESULTS IN THE LEAST AMOUNT OF TIME.**

Born in Southern California, I grew up in middle-class suburbia amidst the backdrop of the California sun and surf culture, and I would not have had it any other way. It was a great life. I find it interesting now, looking back, that when I observed the adults in my world, I couldn't help but think there had to be a better, healthier way to age. No one over 40 seemed remotely fit. I am certain now that this takeaway is how my journey into health and fitness began. It was the catalyst that fueled my interest and passion for finding a superior way to live this amazing life we have been given.

It is shockingly paradoxical how, in a society saturated with health and fitness advice, boasting a gym on seemingly every street corner, our population is witnessing an unprecedented surge in obesity. Despite the constant influx of new diets and revolutionary products promising the ideal physique, the reality is starkly contrary. Our culture's struggle and obsession with weight has reached alarming levels. It's not surprising, is it, that *losing weight is the #1 New Year's resolution* every single year?

For example, this paradox is particularly evident in the persistent rise in diabetes, a condition that could effectively be managed through the right exercise and simple dietary changes. Astonishingly, even with an abundance of information, one in three adults will find themselves succumbing to this debilitating disease. This is a testament to the pressing need for a fundamental shift in our approach to health and fitness. A protocol that is simple, approachable, and sustainable for the average person.

With all I observed and learned in my years in the fitness industry, it was a natural result for me to develop a passion to *educate, inspire, motivate and equip* people to build their best body in order to live their best life. I was tired of seeing people work harder and harder for less and less results. We all have more important things to do with our time, like developing relationships with family and friends, helping others, and building a business, rather than spending countless hours training and being consumed with how to stay fit. For some, it almost becomes a part-time job that you don't get paid for! That is why I crafted a solution that will make fitness simple, efficient, and remarkably effective. If you are tired of wasting your valuable time and not getting the results you work hard for, stay with me.

Imagine achieving better results in a mere **16 MINUTES A DAY**, rather than countless hours at the gym every week (not to mention the drive time), with no need for a gym and very little gear. Yes, it's possible, and I am here to show you how. Through my years of experience and extensive research in exercise science, I've developed the **KBFIT** Training Protocol – a groundbreaking approach designed to deliver maximum results in the shortest amount of time that anyone can do.

Together, we'll embark on a transformative journey where fitness becomes a sustainable and rewarding part of your life. Gone are the days of confusion and wasted effort. My goal is to equip you with a simple program where you will experience a new level of convenience, confidence, and empowerment. Your body will *shift, adapt, and change* as you break through plateaus, build muscle, blast fat, and optimally train your heart, **ALL AT THE SAME TIME!**

I promise to guide you through a fitness revolution. Embrace the joy of reclaiming your time, reshaping your body, and unlocking your true potential. With the **KBFIT** Training Protocol, you can look your best, feel your best, and perform your best – all within 16 minutes a day and without the need for a traditional gym setting. Are you ready to unleash your best self? If so, let's embark on this life-changing journey together.

Firstly, I encourage all my clients to sit down and identify and clarify two crucial aspects of their fitness journey:

#1 – Clearly define their goals – **WHAT** exactly do they want to achieve?

#2 – Delve deeper into the motivations behind those goals – **WHY** do they desire them?

WHAT and WHY: It is essential to ingrain these answers in your mind and revisit them regularly. They will serve as the bedrock of your desire and determination when faced with distractions. When life becomes challenging, when you have time constraints, simply because you don't feel like it, or really important things like you need to fold the laundry or walk the dog, sometimes your mind will come up with any excuse. Your **WHAT and WHY** will keep you anchored.

Consider this: is there anything worth exchanging for your health and fitness? I find it challenging to be able to think of anything, don't you? Without your health and fitness, all other aspirations pale in significance; you cannot fully realize your potential or lead the fulfilling life you deserve. Becoming the best version of yourself not only serves you best but everyone else in your life as well. **The only one that can stop you in YOU!**

So how do we get there? How do we get started, and more importantly, how do we maintain and sustain it? At the outset, I would like to emphasize that I promote principles, not rules. Having said that, this is the principle I follow because it allows me to live a 'normal life' instead of rigid and extreme rules. I follow the **80/20**

Rule. Get it right 80% of the time and you're golden! Success never requires that you do anything perfectly. Perfection does not exist. Embarking on a journey to optimal health and fitness involves understanding and embracing the *three fundamental keys* to both achievement and sustainability. Let's dive into it and discover these simple keys that will unlock a lifetime of wellness and vitality. While the path may not always be easy, the rewards are immeasurable. Most people will find excuses for why they can't, but if you have read this far, *you are not most people. Congratulations!!* Here we go.

Key #1: Master Your Mindset

Optimal and sustainable fitness is not solely manifested in physical exertion or dietary choices – it originates fundamentally from the power of your mind. Your thoughts and beliefs are the driving force behind transforming your body. If you believe you can achieve it – IT'S YOURS! By reshaping and retraining your mindset, you empower yourself step-by-step into a transformative journey, creating your best self. *So fitness does not begin with your training; it does not begin with the food on your plate; IT BEGINS IN YOUR MIND.* You must actually start to identify yourself as a fit person, even if you are not where you want to be yet. What does a fit person do? How does a fit person think? How does a fit person act? *THINK FIT, ACT FIT, BE FIT.* Your mind will be your best asset in transforming your body.

KEY #2: FOOD MANAGEMENT vs DIETING. Never 'diet' again.

The notion of 'dieting' implies short-term restrictions. Instead, *simply focus on managing your food intake for long-term sustainability based on how you want to look and feel.* Admittedly, food is not just about sustenance; it also plays a pivotal role in our emotional connections, cultural traditions, and social interactions. Embrace a food philosophy that promotes balance without deprivation, allowing you to enjoy social gatherings and culinary pleasures without sacrificing your short and long-term health and fitness goals.

Most of us consume far more food energy than our bodies need. Become attuned to your body's true needs and avoid overindulging out of habit or emotional cravings. Take charge of your food choices. Empower yourself to eat for nourishment, along with pleasure, without succumbing to mindless consumption that gets you nowhere but fat. Harness the power of *conscious eating* to fuel your body and mind, turning food into a source of vitality and energy rather than a source of guilt or restriction. It's time to break up with your dysfunctional relationship with food.

Does anyone force you to eat anything? The truth is, you are always in control, whether it feels like it or not. Here are a few good questions to ask: Why am I eating this? How will it make me look? How will it make me feel? *Simply make choices based on how you want to look and feel.*

Remember, the control over your dietary decisions ultimately resides with you. Be selective and eat by design instead of default. Actually, nothing is off-limits. You can eat some of whatever you want; you just can't overeat it. Never put anything in your mouth that you haven't made a conscious choice to do so. *You can't out-train a bad diet!* And never allow people or a social situation to coerce you into indulging. Always make choices in your best interest. By adopting a sustainable food philosophy that aligns with your well-being, you will liberate yourself from the cycles of both restrictive dieting as well as the dysfunction of overeating.

Since we live in the real world, there will be times you will go off the rails, as we all do. Here is my advice. Cut your losses quickly and minimize any perceived setback. Refocus and course correct. Don't dwell on any poor choices you made – it's already done, you can't change it. What you can change and control is what you do next. Let this new perspective on how to manage your food guide you toward lasting transformation and a future free from the constraints of traditional diets. You will never need them again!

Key #3: The Training Magic.

Yes, it is magic. I say this in all seriousness because I am thoroughly convinced that this is the case, and that is what lights me up –sharing it with others! It changed my life. It can change yours. ***CHANGING YOUR LIFE IS THE PRIZE!***

The right training protocol will make you look great, but it is about far more than just looking good. It will not only transform your body into the best version of yourself, it will actually make you **biologically younger.** How cool is that?! I call it *'the elixir of youth'*, and for good reason. Beyond extending your life, it will give you a much higher quality of life. If you could put it into a pill, everyone would want it, and everyone would take it – guaranteed. But you can actually do it in 16 minutes a day and create that magic for yourself. Who doesn't want to look better, feel better, move better, perform better, and live a longer, healthier life with less disease and dysfunction? ***Our goal should be to die young, as late as possible.*** Training with the right protocol will do just that!

Throw out the old, outdated model of having to spend hours working out. Get rid of the notion that you have to go to a gym. Discard thinking you need some special, expensive fancy gear. People have made it complicated, confusing and time consuming for a reason. That should become obvious as you keep reading along.

What if I told you that you could get all your training done at once, in only 16 minutes a day? What if I told you that you would get far better results in far less time and you could do it anywhere and anytime? What if you could optimally blast fat, especially belly fat, maximally train your heart, gain balance and agility, and build muscle, *ALL AT THE SAME TIME in mere minutes?* Who wouldn't want to? ***I would! You would! We all would!***

I know people who go to the gym on a regular basis, and their bodies never change. The truth is that some types of exercise actually trigger the body to store fat. But they keep doing it. They keep spending countless hours every week, just like I did before. I knew better and made a breakthrough with **KBFIT.** People act as if they don't care how much time they spend doing their workouts. However, once you understand how valuable and limited your time is, the only reasonable conclusion is to make your training time as efficient and effective as possible to get the best results in the least amount of time.

The science is clearly coming down now for quite some time on the side of short, intense training using your own bodyweight in interval mode to be far superior to traditional training models. I switched over and launched my **KBFIT** program a decade ago. I never train more than 12 minutes a day, and my physique is better than it was fifteen years ago. Allow me to mention just a few very important benefits that you will want to know about.

HGH, the human growth hormone, also known as the 'fountain of youth hormone,' is critical to keeping the body strong and lean and the mind vibrant and youthful. HGH peaks at puberty and then escalates into a rapid decline along with the aging process. Increasing HGH levels has proven to be very difficult. The wealthy pay upwards of $1,000 a week for HGH injections, but they are not without risk. Believe it or not, another way to get a significant HGH release that not a lot of people know about is from ***short-duration, high-intensity training.*** I can offer you just that, at a far reduced rate! Now that's a bargain! And an anti-aging hack you can take to the bank that will turn back the clock if you commit to doing it consistently over time.

Insulin sensitivity is foundational to being healthy, fit, and lean. Almost half of the adult population is considered obese, increasing the risk of chronic disease, insulin resistance being one of them. Insulin resistance, if left unchecked, wears out the pancreas and leads to type II diabetes. Diabetes can be a debilitating disease that is projected to increase by 54% by 2030, just a few short years away. Guess which type of exercise studies show improves insulin sensitivity and reduces type II diabetes? Yes, you are right! **High-intensity, short-duration workouts** improve glucose metabolism, causing the deterioration of insulin resistance. In other words, if you want to stave off diabetes, you need to start doing it yesterday.

Mitochondria. If you are not familiar, you need to be. **Mitochondria are the Powerhouse of Your Body.** They play a critical role in our general health, specifically when it comes to aging. The health of your mitochondria actually determines how your body handles the aging process. A prominent theory again holds that the decaying of mitochondria is a key driver of aging. If you could do something that would enhance and improve your mitochondria, was super convenient, easy to fit into your lifestyle, took just mere minutes a day, and was the cost of a cup of coffee per week, would you do it? Of course, you would! One type of exercise is revolutionary when it comes to mitochondria enhancement, which actually makes you biologically younger! ***Short, intense exercise*** that places a big demand on your system is a major stimulator to increase **MITOCHONDRIAL DENSITY.** Within 24 hours of MAX intensity exercise, new mitochondria are being formed, effectively stopping aging at the cellular level. This is one reason it is critical that you train with intensity and why one of my taglines is ***TRAIN STRONGER, NOT LONGER!*** Hence, *KBFIT2020.com!*

You have the opportunity to unlock a future brimming with vibrancy, resilience, and enduring youthfulness that most people are not aware of. If you could be anything in life, wouldn't you want to be the best version of yourself? The choice is yours. Is it easy? No. Is it worth it? ***Absolutely, and it will Change Your Life!***

***

KBFIT by Karen Butler www.kbfit2020.com

https://www.instagram.com/kbfit20/

https://www.facebook.com/karen.butler.5209

www.linkedin.com/in/kbfit-by-karen-butler-01394166

KBFIT20@outlook.com

Lisa Burns

I am a spit-fire Latina from the *barrio* that has been saved by the grace of God. I have felt hopeless, unworthy and overwhelmed by life. It is only through embracing that pain that healing took place. Our greatest adversity is what sets us up for our greatest purpose in life. I am an Executive Level Trauma Coach, a Positive Behavior Facilitator for the school district, a motivational speaker and an educational trainer. I speak messages of hope, healing and finding your life spark. I am passionate about training educators on how to work with students of trauma, mental illness and those that struggle with emotional regulation. I speak at events to inspire, encourage and empower others to take hold of their irreplaceable role in this world, without hindrances. Unbreakable joy is possible, regardless of your situation. It is not based on circumstances. Regardless of trauma, illness, death, heartbreak, or mental health, you can rise back up. Do you feel stuck in life and know you are not reaching your greatest potential? Join me in being a life changer, fulfilling your dreams passionately and leaving a legacy.

Beauty From Ashes

By Lisa Burns

I've spent half of my life running from the trauma of a past that would never leave me. At a very early age, the world had already shown me how brutal it could be. I was in a small town in Maine that was not welcoming to our brown skinned family. At least living in the barrio, we were surrounded by the struggle. This place taught me that racism is more of a verb than a noun. I saw it, I heard it, I was struck by it every day. Before I knew *who* I was, I was told *what* I was. Their hateful words became my inner voice that shaped my identity.

For five years, we lived in the unfinished basement of a house with cold, dark, damp cement walls. One small window sat right above the grass line where light from the outside slipped in. The only other source of light came from a bulb that hung from a cord dropped through a hole in the ceiling. We didn't have plumbing, so we had a bucket in the corner that served as our restroom. Every few days, my mother would walk through the woods a half a mile to a well to fill a bucket of water to bring back to us. We ate mostly canned food, and we were thankful for it. I didn't even complain that I had to curl my toes under to make my shoes fit. I was simply grateful. I wouldn't know for years to come of the damage the black mold had done inside my brain, or how the lack of sunlight had caused weakness in my muscles and bones, a depletion of vitamin D and cognitive fatigue. By 8 years old, I already felt weighted down by all the things happening in my life.

When we finally moved back to my mom's side of the family in Roswell, New Mexico, I had completely lost touch with my Mexican heritage. Being mixed left you in the middle of nowhere. I didn't look white enough to fit into that culture, so I thought once I went back to the people who looked like me, I'd finally be accepted. For years, I had been inundated with the message that "Mexicans are the dogs of the earth", and now that I was immersed back into my other culture, I realized very quickly that I no longer fit in there either. I couldn't speak Spanish, didn't understand the traditions, and didn't understand why I had to have a label of "what" I was. I was just a girl, in a big swirling world, trying to find a place to just be me. In school, I was so far behind that I couldn't catch up. I didn't understand basic concepts and had such a fear of failure, I eventually shut down. Not even lunch and recess gave me any kind of relief. I was completely out of the loop socially. Since we didn't have a television, radio, or any other link to the outside world, I couldn't relate to most of the conversations about shows, music, toys, or any of the other things that were relevant. When I would ask questions, I would get laughed at for not knowing "normal" things everyone else knew. The phrase, "Did you grow up under a rock?" could have literally been written about me. I became a select mute and was retained because they thought I wasn't capable of learning. All this did was make me feel more isolated and I withdrew even deeper inside myself.

My brother had always been my protector. Shortly after we moved back, he was recruited into one of the most violent gangs in existence. One thing life had taught him at an early age was how to take a hit. He was one of the best fighters I had ever seen. He did everything he could to shield me from that world, but when someone in your family is in a gang, your life expectancy drastically decreases. While other kids were running track in school, my brother was teaching me how to do an evasive 10-yard jump and dash. *"Mi Vida Loca"* was a phrase we embraced, until it all went up in flames. My brother caught his first case and was in and out of lock up for the next several years. This left me unprotected from the chaos. Unable to cope, I fell into a deep depression. I remember sitting in school wondering why I even tried anymore. I had already been tracked in that school as someone who wasn't expected to graduate so most of my classes consisted of electives. In one of those classes, my teacher asked us to write about what we wanted to be when we grew up. I sat staring at that paper until the bell rang for dismissal, then I wrote one word.

"Alive."

I just wanted a chance to be alive long enough to grow up. And yet, at 16, I decided I had experienced all this world had to offer and was done suffering. My life consisted of physical, sexual, and mental abuse. I had been sexually assaulted 5 different times. I had attended so many friend's funerals that I didn't even cry over loss anymore. I felt numb unless I was self-harming. I was breathing, but I wasn't living. I saw the path in front of me and knew the only way out of this world of pain was in a box. So, as an 80-pound anorexic teen, I downed a bottle of Tylenol with codeine. I've heard that most people regret their attempt at suicide, but I began my descent in the 10% that welcomed it…that is until I began to wonder if there was life after death. What if my late grandmother's words were true? What if there was a God? What if there was a Heaven and a Hell? In those last moments where I could feel my body beginning to float and darkness closing in on me, I was pierced with fear. I cried out in my last few breaths,

"God, if you are real, please save me. I have already lived through hell, and I can't take it anymore. I have nothing to offer you, but please let me be with you."

As soon as I uttered those words, I saw a bright light, heard His voice, and felt a warm sensation course through my body like a warm blanket being wrapped around me. For the first time in my life, I was encircled by a sense of peace that I can't explain in words, and I let go of this world as I knew it.

I woke up the next day, in the same place on the floor, staring up at the same ceiling I had said goodbye to. I knew it was impossible for me to survive an overdose of that much codeine, so my first thought was, "Oh Lord, I'm in Hell." But then, I felt this searing pain in my chest. My mind began to race with thoughts of what was happening to my body. Amid my panic, I heard a now familiar voice inside me say,

"That is what love feels like when it has to break through a hardened heart."

From that moment until now, my heart and mind have been forever changed. I knew that, against all odds, He had saved me. Before I knew Him, He had known me. Some might argue that near death experiences cause hallucinations. What I can tell you is that I know I had a supernatural experience that began to mend my shattered heart, renew my hope, and speak into me that I was to be a light in the darkness. That is the day I started living life knowing I had a divine purpose.

I changed my mantra from *Mi Vida Loca* to *Make It Matter*. I had survived traumatic experiences yet had let the memory of it slowly suck the life out of me. I was hiding all the trauma of my past with a mask of humor and this façade that I was unshakeable. While I presented myself as this fun, outgoing, optimistically lighthearted person that others wanted to be around, inside, I was constantly trying not to drown and overanalyzing everything I said and did.

My new healing journey started with being willing to embrace the real me. I was optimistic, but also felt things deeply. I was outgoing, but also needed time to be alone to process all my thoughts and experiences. I loved making people laugh, but only allowed my pillow to hold my tears. I strived for this idealistic happiness that wasn't achievable. When I learned to accept this multifaceted version of myself, I had an epiphany that joy is a choice. It is not based on circumstances, nor on what you have or don't have. My joy comes from my refusal to be overcome by the things of this world. My joy is set in the foundation of my faith. As long as I can stand out in the open and toss my head back to take in the beauty of the sunlight, I am BLESSED.

I used to think I had a fear of failure, but what I really had was a fear of success. Expectations of me were already set low. Breaking through that glass ceiling is where the grit had to kick in. I had to expand my mindset. Statistically, I was destined to fail as a minority that came from a broken family, living in poverty, academically disadvantaged, with mental illness and addiction that plagued several of my family members on both sides. I had watched so many go down a path I dreaded. Deaths by suicide and gang life, drop out and crime rates were all steadily increasing. If I wanted a different kind of life, I had to be willing to do things differently. I had to be brave, step out and take big risks. I had to have the discipline, commitment, and resilience to overcome every adversity life brought to me. I noticed the correlation of the trajectory of those around me that had dropped out of school, and it led to the kind of life I did not want. So, I did the opposite. I became one of the first in my family to finish high school and graduate from college. In the summers, I did youth internships at inner-city churches. I realized how much of an impact I could make if I had more time to work with our youth, so I chose a career in education. I moved to Dallas,

Texas and worked at a Title I campus with at-risk students and loved every minute of it. I started a Step Team, an organization for students that had trauma, and mentoring groups. I had a food pantry, clothes pantry and amazing volunteers that donated Christmas gifts for every one of my students for years. I created a social-emotional curriculum to teach coping skills and healthy boundaries. My classroom was set up like a living room and we were not just a class, we were a family. I thrived in that environment, but it wasn't enough. There was so much pain and chaos in the world, I needed to do more. I was involved with the apartment community where my students lived, and I recruited some friends to help me set up games and lunch for them a few times in the summer. When I wasn't doing that, I jumped into going on mission trips. I went to Skid Row, Harlem and Honduras to work with street kids. I loved it, but I felt like I was just putting on a band aid and not actually bringing a solution for others to get out of poverty, and to deal with the abuse and trauma they were experiencing. Since I was not equipped or trained, aside from life experience, I knew I needed to add more knowledge to my toolbox. I attended a Life Coaching Institute with Dr. Neecie Moore and became certified as a Life Coach, then a Master Life Coach and then the highest level I could reach as an Executive Level Trauma Coach. I modified what I had learned in this training into kid friendly lessons and began to introduce these social and coping skills into my morning meetings every day. I started a monthly parent night where I would coach parents through this curriculum to use on their own. I also took on a few clients who had experienced trauma and worked with them after school and on the weekends. When I realized that I didn't have the bandwidth to take on more than a few clients at a time, I then became involved in training other life coaches so our impact could be greater. I also started doing campus and district trainings to equip educators on how to create safe spaces for students of trauma to thrive. After 20 years of teaching, I transitioned to a Positive Behavior Facilitator where I work with students in the district who have maladaptive behavior, and I teach them coping skills. Throughout all of this, there was still a hole in my soul. A dear friend had been coaching me on not just throwing myself into helping others heal, but to also release myself from the bondage of my own past. I never wanted to see myself as a victim because it made me feel weak and vulnerable.

But being a victim doesn't mean you have to stay there. Once you come to terms with the pain and how it has shaped you, you can change the unhealthy aspects of it to move into living as an overcomer. This friend began to encourage me to live out the "Make It Matter" motto I had taken on. If I could share my story with others, then maybe they wouldn't feel so alone and see that it is possible to break free from limiting beliefs. I started speaking at different conferences, seminars, and retreats. After every event, especially ones in the Christian arena, I heard the same comments. So many people shared about how they were stuck in their life circumstances and needed a breakthrough. We have grown so much in being trauma informed, but there needed to be more to prepare others to go beyond the trauma to deal, heal and release it. I began teaching a course in our church called Emotional Wellbeing, Boundaries and Forgiveness. We also need a tribe. One of the greatest support systems I have is my connection to an inner circle of people who keep me accountable and cheer me on. They are my lifelong friends, and I would not be who or where I am today without them.

All the "things" I have done are in vain without love. So, I leave you with my most important life message; I am not some extraordinary person. I am simply a person who was given a chance to tell my story because my great God saved me. Everything I have done came from the roots of my wounds. I became the very thing I needed others to be for me. This is how I changed adversity into opportunity. Without the mess of my life, I would not have the life spark that I do. I have devoted my life to speaking words of empowerment into the hopeless, love to those who feel they are unlovable and truth to those that have accepted a tainted view of themselves. I am an advocate of positive change. I am a protector to those who cannot protect themselves. There is no situation, no circumstance, no mistake that can take away your value. Stop letting your wounds define you, use them to propel you. You are worthy. Your life matters. This world is better because you are in it. Those who intended you harm may have taken from your past, but they cannot have your future, unless you give it to them. Love yourself enough to become unbound and free. How? Forgive them. Yes, you heard me right. I have been beaten, raped, left barren, abandoned, misused, betrayed and broken more times than I can count. And I'm STILL standing. But, hating them was keeping me in a cage. Forgiveness doesn't mean what they did was okay; it doesn't release them from responsibility. Just as holding on to your anger doesn't bring meaning to it because they're out living their life while you stay trapped. It is time. Right now, this is your time. Release yourself from this burden and let go of how it has held you back for too long. You were created to shine. You are valuable, resilient and irreplaceable. I know what it feels like when your whole world has been burned down. I am a living testimony that beauty can come from ashes. Get back up, brush yourself off, get you a circle of support, do the work it takes to heal and then turn around and help the next person do the same thing. That is how we change this world together.

I hope you join me in living in gratitude and joy, rising back up and being a beacon of hope to those around you. It's never too late. What have you given up on, or hidden, that you are willing to unveil to reach a passionate place of purpose? What legacy will you leave?

If you or someone you know needs help overcoming whatever is holding them back from living life joyfully, please send them to my website. I would love to hear from you, whether that is to share your story or give feedback. You can also book me for an event, training or sign up for a coaching package.

www.unbreakablejoy.com

lisaburnsjoy@gmail.com

Facebook: @lisaburns50 and @unbreakablejoy1

TikTok and Instagram: @lbsmilez

Youtube: @lbsmilez1

Eric C. Weaver

Eric Weaver is a leading expert, advocate, speaker, and instructor on mental health issues, specializing in law enforcement. He is a retired sergeant with the Rochester, NY Police Dept., where he served from 1985-2005. He was a police sergeant for the RPD for the last 13 years of his career. He also served as a Corrections Officer from 1983-1985 with in Upstate NY. His last assignment for the Rochester Police Department was as Mental Health Coordinator, and was the creator, developer, and Commanding Officer of the first Crisis Intervention Team in NYS.

In 2010, Eric developed and began directing his own full-time training and consulting business, "Overcoming the Darkness", in which he provides internationally recognized certification programs, training seminars and keynote addresses on recovery, mental illness, stigmas, communication skills, and suicide awareness, prevention and intervention, for law enforcement agencies, mental health counselors and agencies, hospitals, schools, colleges, and consumer and community groups.

Diagnosed with severe mental illness and hospitalized for suicidality on numerous occasions between 1996 and 2023, Eric openly and honestly shares his story with each of his audiences. In 2002, after the suicide death of a fellow RPD officer, he wrote and developed his seminar, 'Overcoming The Darkness," a course on mental health, cumulative stress, stigmas, depression, PTSD, suicide prevention and awareness within law enforcement and among officers themselves.

Overcoming The Darkness: Shining light on Mental Illness, Trauma, and Suicide in Law Enforcement.

By Sgt. Eric Weaver (Ret.)

All my life I wanted to be a police officer, which is why my parents would always find me spending time at the NYS Police exhibit at the State Fair. As a young teen I joined the NYS Police Explorers Program, which eventually led to working in campus security at nineteen. In 1983, while just a twenty-year-old kid, I started working in law enforcement in a maximum-security county jail in Upstate NY.

So, there I was at twenty years old with a uniform, working in a particularly challenging culture of law enforcement-corrections. A culture like no other and all unto itself. After I worked in corrections, in 1985 I was hired by the Rochester, NY Police Department. Going from a correction's officer to a police officer was challenging.

In 1986 after the academy, I worked patrol in Rochester until 1992 when I was promoted to the rank of sergeant. Little did I know that in just three years of being promoted, my life and career would be forever changed.

"If I don't tell you something, I'm going to kill myself." Those words were said to my then wife in the fall of 1995. At that time, I was the training coordinator for our SWAT team, as well as a sniper and entry team leader. I commanded my own platoon of proactive, hard charging officers. Given my very tough exterior, the words I said to my wife that day were hard for her to hear, and even harder for me to say. She immediately said that I should get help. I told her that I would, but that she was in no way to tell anyone what I had told her. After all, what would people say if they found out that I, Sgt. Eric Weaver, was seriously contemplating killing himself? Against all odds and setting aside arrogant pride, I reached out for help. I called my primary care doctor, and although I was never direct with him about how I was feeling, he connected me with a counselor shortly thereafter.

After I started seeing my therapist, my overwhelming sense of depression and suicide reached a level that I could no longer manage. In the spring of 1996, I had to admit that I was as close to suicide as I could be. I was not safe at work nor at home, and it was determined that the only thing I could do to stay safe was to be hospitalized.

I was not thrilled at the thought of being in a psychiatric hospital. After all, I've worked with and responded to mentally ill people who are in crisis on the job for years, and I certainly didn't feel like I was one of "those people." However, the fact remained that I was sure to die if I wasn't hospitalized. I went to a hospital well outside of Rochester where, given my extremely depressed and suicidal condition, it was decided I was to be admitted. I was devastated, not sure what was happening to me, and wishing I had never told anyone about how I was feeling.

Of course, before being hospitalized that day, I had to call in sick to work. But what would I say? I certainly couldn't tell the person who answered the phone at work that I was in a psychiatric hospital. We all know if that was said, word would spread fast throughout the department. So that wasn't even an option. I just said I had a back injury from working out-no stigma there.

I stayed in the hospital for about one week. It was not the most pleasant of places, but it kept me safe and alive, for the time being at least. After I was discharged, I was sent home and was given a treatment plan to follow up with some doctors for counseling and medication. I figured I could handle that, even though I didn't want to. So, as I sat home the following week with my "back injury," I began to realize that my depression and thoughts of suicide were not going away, and in fact they were just getting worse.

Shortly after my discharge, I found myself in the bathroom of my home. I had locked myself in, banging my head against the toilet, and was trying to cut my head open with the skeleton key that was above the door frame.

Once my wife realized that I was hurting myself in the bathroom- thankful today that I didn't have my gun with me in that room- she immediately called my therapist, who then called 911. You can probably imagine my anger when I was told that the police were being called on me. After all, how would someone expect a very mean, angry, depressed, suicidal SWAT team sergeant to react? I yelled through the bathroom door that "if some rookie deputy sheriff showed up, that they better bring a bunch of them as no one was going to take me out of my own home." Of course, these were words that I had heard hundreds of times from other people in crisis while on the job, but now it was me who was saying them.

The police responded, and I refused to come out of the bathroom. I yelled that the only way that I was going to come out was if my captain came to my home and ordered me out. My wife called him, and he immediately came to my home and ordered me to come out of the bathroom. I did and was taken back to the hospital for another admission. In the spring and summer of 1996, I was hospitalized a total of five times, eventually being admitted to a hospital in Rochester on three of those occasions. I underwent intense treatment that summer, including various medications and even ECT, electroconvulsive therapy, for my treatment-resistant depression.

As you might imagine, life was hard. Believe it or not, I was able to return to work in the beginning of fall 1996. Of course, I needed medical clearance and approval from our police physician, who was very understanding and empathetic to what I had been going through. Besides my family, work was all I had. I had been a police officer since I was twenty years old. I needed to come back to work to feel whole again. On the first day back at work I was nervous as to what was going to be said to me. You can imagine my relief when I kept getting the same question over and over. "So, Sarge, how's your back?" I couldn't believe it! I had been in and out of psychiatric hospitals five times, out of work for nearly six months, and my confidentiality had been kept.

For the next couple of years, I seemed to flourish. I was back working on SWAT and had been hand selected for our Tactical Unit. Again, life seemed good. Unfortunately, my behavior wasn't. I had to prove to myself that I wasn't just some crazy guy who had been locked up in psychiatric hospitals. My behavior had gotten so out of control that I found myself in the spring of 1998 facing some pretty serious internal departmental charges. Eventually everything that I thought I was, was taken from me. I was removed from the SWAT team, the Tactical Unit, suspended for fifteen days, and removed entirely from patrol to serve time on administrative duty for one full year. The only thing I was allowed to retain was my rank. I felt that life was now officially over.

While on administrative duty one day during the summer of 1998, I sat quietly alone in the basement of our public safety building telling myself that this was it and the time had come. My life as I had known it was over, I could no longer fight anymore, and I no longer desired to go on with my life. I sat on a bench in the far corner of the men's locker room with my department issued Beretta 9mm handgun in my hand for about the 50th time. I was alone and I was determined that this was how and where I would die. I figured everyone would now learn how much I was hurting inside.

The images of my family passed through my mind briefly; how they would take the news, how the funeral would go, who would be there, and if anyone would even care that I was dead. These images had passed through my mind hundreds of times over the years, but this time seemed different. With my gun in my hand, I was gently pulling back the trigger when I heard the faint sounds of someone walking in the door and then into the restroom area of the locker room. The locker room was very large with a hundred lockers, and even though I was sitting as far away from the entrance as I could get, I could still hear what sounded like water running in one of the sinks. I didn't want anyone around when I killed myself. This was personal, and I wanted to be alone.

So, I quickly put my gun back in my holster, got up, and started walking through the locker room. With great disappointment and frustration that I didn't go through with my suicide, I walked out of the locker room fully expecting to see one of my fellow officers washing his hands. However, there was no one at the sink. In fact, I saw no one at all. I figured I must have just been hearing things. But now, since no one was in the bathroom, I was faced with two choices-I could go back and finish what I came to the locker room to do or leave. For whatever reason, I chose to leave. Remarkably, I didn't kill myself that day in 1998 because of the sounds of running water from a sink. I would discover many years later what God's plans were for me in my life, and they didn't include killing myself in a police locker room that day. I then called my wife and told her what had happened and later that day I admitted myself to the same psychiatric hospital I had been in two years before. Believe it or not, I would be back to work again in just a few short weeks.

Life after that last discharge and my administrative assignment wasn't too bad. I was back to work on patrol, and once again, no one knew where I really was for all that time I was not working. I was still seeing a therapist and still taking medications to help in my recovery. It was around the summer of 2000 that my life took a huge turn. Up until then, I was a very devout atheist. And that all changed that year when I allowed God into my life. Many people might stop reading at this point for fear I'm going to be preachy. After all, I know I would have thought that back then as well. But I would be remiss if I didn't share this part of my story- as it changed my life.

In 2002, I was forever changed again when I experienced the loss of a fellow police officer, Eddie Martinez, to suicide. I had worked with Eddie as a fellow officer and then as his sergeant. Eddie had been going through divorce proceedings with his wife and child custody disputes, as well as a variety of other things, which caused him to take his own life. When I heard of Eddie's death, I knew immediately that I had to share my story of my depression, mental illness, suicidality, and hospitalizations with my department. I figured that if I was able to share my story with my fellow officers, maybe I could help save a life.

I knew I had to do something. So, I asked my supervisor for 10 minutes on the command staff's meeting agenda to share with them what I had gone through. As I was waiting for my turn to speak, I was building up the courage to share with them all that I had been hiding for too long. When it was my turn, I let it all come out. I told the staff that we have officers who are struggling with so much, now on the brink of suicide. I asked if I could put something together to teach at our in-service regarding my story as well as the topics of stigma, cumulative stress, trauma, suicide, and some tips and resources they could refer themselves to.

Most of the command staff were taken aback by my story. I had one captain tell me in no uncertain terms that I could not get up in front of seven hundred officers and tell them I was in a psychiatric hospital six times. I asked him why, and he gave me an answer that will stick with me forever. He said, "Sergeant, this is all well and good that you want to share your story, but what would people say?" I said to him, "Captain, that's the problem. We are so concerned about what a bunch of people may think of us that we are willing to throw away our families, careers, and now our very lives. I have been on the job for 17 years, and if people don't like me by now, they are not going to."

That is when I started speaking on mental health. I continued to speak openly about my mental health challenges and various diagnoses. Prior to retiring, I spoke openly with numerous organizations, sharing my story of mental illness in full uniform. In 2003, another opportunity for change in my career arose. I was charged with creating, implementing, and instructing the first Crisis Intervention Team (CIT) in NYS. I ran numerous classes up until retirement in 2005 and have taught countless CIT training courses throughout NYS. After people heard my story, I was asked to do keynote speeches around the country about my personal journey and recovery. After all, how many officers talk openly about their mental illnesses?

When I retired in 2005, I entered ministry, but that didn't miraculously take my mental illnesses away. My suicidality once again became so overwhelming that I was then hospitalized, as a pastor, in 2008.

I have trained and have spoken to thousands of law enforcement officers and other first responders for the last two decades. Whether it be a keynote address to five hundred officers, a room of ten, or one on one conversations over a cup of coffee. I have helped countless officers who are living with or struggling with severe mental health and substance abuse issues. In 2006, I was hired by the Rochester Psychiatric Center as a peer support specialist, and a few years later as the Western NY coordinator for the Western NY Chapter of the American Foundation for Suicide Prevention. In 2013, I became a national trainer with the National Council on Behavioral Health (now the National Council of Mental Wellness), an extensive course on the issues of mental health challenges and crisis, and I also assisted with writing one of the courses related to training public safety officers.

After my hospitalization in 2008, I started my own training and consulting business titled *Overcoming the Darkness* with a tag line of "Shining Light on the Issues of Mental illness, Trauma, and Suicide" which is the same title of my 2021 book, which is specific to law enforcement and their families. I still fight battles every day. My mental illness and severe suicidality caused me to be hospitalized three more times 2014, in 2017, where I spent time at a Trauma Disorders Center in Baltimore, and with my last hospitalization during the week of Easter in 2023, all for a grand total of 10 hospitalizations.

Coaching law enforcement and other first responders is now what I am being called to do. I have worked with not only the officers themselves but with their families. Trying to figure out how to deal with a suffering loved one who works in these particularly challenging professions - whether it be spouse, parent, sibling, or child - is a constant struggle for many. Even though more officers are getting help than before, the culture of law enforcement is not conducive to actually getting help. I know of officers who have been suspended or fired for having a mental health challenge and that, of course, needs to change.

Law enforcement is demanding work, and thankfully not every officer is thinking about suicide. But substance abuse, divorce rates, heart disease, severe cumulative stress and burnout, and untreated and undiagnosed PTSD are prevalent. I have dedicated my life to helping law enforcement officers. A profession that needs help, not criticism. A profession that needs understanding and care, not a profession that people throw stones at, literally and figuratively. I want to be there to coach officers and first responders to reach their life goals and encourage them to seek professional help whenever necessary.

My journey through life as a law enforcement officer, as a pastor, and now as a mental health trainer and police consultant, as well as a husband and father, has been filled with every emotion-from total despair and worthlessness to a life filled with hope and purpose. We know that coaching is not counseling and/or therapy, and if that situation arose, I would clearly encourage someone to seek appropriate professional help, but so many officers and first responders do need to discuss the specific and difficult challenges of a very demanding career.

It has been my mission over the last two decades to: reduce stigma; increase understanding surrounding the many challenges of mental health related issues; create a culture that openly discusses the topic of mental illness, suicide, and suicide-related behavior; and above all, proclaim that there is hope and that recovery from mental health challenges are not only possible, but probable. We just need to strongly encourage individuals to get the help they need.

Today, life is actually very good. That is not to say I don't still have my moments. But as I continue to work on my own mental health issues and speak publicly on the aspects of officer wellness, I strive to be a living example that a level of recovery is available to everyone. The law enforcement community struggles with knowing what to do with officers who experience mental health or career development challenges. Police supervisors, of whom many are also desperately in need of life coaching, have a responsibility of assisting officers' challenges and changing police culture, though sadly that rarely happens. We are quick to judge and call officers out that are having a challenging time, labeled as "unfit for duty", when all they need is some coaching and encouragement. Because of my experience, I have a very unique perspective-and one that can help so many.

To contact Eric:

website, www.overcomingthedarkness.com and fill out a request/contact form, or email me directly at eric@overcomingthedarkness.com.

If interested in reading more of my story, as well as further understanding the need for support regarding cumulative stress, trauma, suicide, family, recovery, and career development, please take a look at my book, which is available on Amazon, *'Overcoming the Darkness; Shining Light on the Issues of Mental Illness, Trauma, and Suicide in Law Enforcement."*

The Change [21]

If you or someone you care about is thinking about suicide, please call or text 988.

Jan Davidson

For over 25 years, I've walked the path of recovery; I beat addiction and its grip on my life. That journey, interwoven with navigating trauma and grief, forged a deep understanding of their impact. I know firsthand the struggle to transform debilitating thoughts, emotions, and habits. But here's the truth: change is possible, and within it lies a rediscovered self, a life seen through "fresh, clear" eyes.

This profound personal transformation fueled my passion to guide others through their own journeys. I became equipped to help people move through the change process, proving that stagnation isn't their destiny. As I often say, "With the unwavering support of dedicated professionals who believed in me, I found the strength to invest in myself, and so can you."

In my previous role as the director of addiction recovery services at Indiana Women's Prison, I managed a team of counselors who delivered evidence-based programs for incarcerated women with substance use disorders.

My expertise reflects this commitment. I hold credentials as a CADAC II Addiction Counselor, MATS (Medicated Assisted Treatment Specialist), AGRMS (Advanced Grief Recovery Specialist), CCTSA (Clinical Trauma Specialist-Addiction), a Mindfulness Teacher/Practitioner, SAMSHA Trainer for Trauma-Informed Responses, and a Master Life Coach.

My life purpose: To help people navigate the hills and valleys of their professional and personal lives, while growing through their journey.

Understanding the Behaviors of Grief

By Jan Davidson

Recognizing Grief Beyond the Surface

There is an elephant in the room. Many see and know it is there; it seems easier for many of us to walk around it and allow it space. The elephant makes many people uncomfortable, so they tend to pretend it does not exist. The elephant has a name. Sometimes, we forget it and call it something else. It has the ability to mimic so many different emotions that, at times, it is hard to identify.

The elephant's name is GRIEF.

For more than twenty-five years, grief has been a teacher of mine. I've watched it in my life and the lives of others. These years have allowed me to gain vast knowledge about it through educating myself, experientially working with others, and paying attention to the consistency of my observations.

I've had the privilege of helping grievers working at a homeless shelter, the Indiana Department of Corrections, churches, and individual businesses, along with family and friends.

I began to observe patterns of behavior that were consistent when individuals experienced grief and loss. I took notes, erased them, and took more notes. I also talked to numerous people grieving and watched how grief unfolded in the lives of those around me to evaluate the validity of what I had captured as the behaviors of grief.

Grief is like a fingerprint, unique to each individual it touches. Just as no two fingerprints are alike, no two experiences of grief are the same. It is a deeply personal and complex emotion that can manifest in various ways.

Grief is not a linear process with a clear beginning and end. It is a tangled web of emotions, behaviors, thoughts, and physical sensations that can ebb and flow unpredictably. It can be overwhelming, all-consuming, and sometimes seem impossible to navigate.

Grief is the normal and natural emotional reaction to the loss of ANY kind.

This chapter will provide you with the framework to identify repetitive behaviors that occur when someone experiences a loss; this information will allow you to understand grief better and engage with a griever better because you are more familiar with how grief behaves.

Reacting to Grief

Studying individuals experiencing grief has been an educational and enlightening privilege for me. Inevitably, every person has a reaction as they learn about a loss. Interestingly, there is no way to predict how a person will absorb the information and react to it. Initially, your emotional self normally takes over and will drive the "quick reaction" and determine the first feedback you display.

You may find yourself going through the motions, mechanically moving through the moment or the day as if on autopilot. The news of the loss may numb your senses, creating a bubble around you and insulating you from the outside world. It's a defense mechanism, a coping strategy to buy yourself time to process the news.

Observing grievers has allowed me to witness a barrage of reactions. You cannot categorize them based on the type of loss that occurred; you cannot sort them by age, race, socioeconomic status, language, or culture.

Internally, emotions can swirl like a turbulent sea. Fear, anger, confusion, numbness, bewilderment of the present reality, and even denial can emerge. Others may withdraw or become stoic. Busyness engulfs some, and they begin to accelerate into activity. Anger has different faces and is displayed in many ways. Each time a person gets angry, it does not present itself similarly.

You may catch yourself clinging to the hope that this is all just a bad dream, that you will wake up and everything will return to normal. But reality is persistent and will continue to remind you of your present grief.

As you navigate this difficult terrain, remember that feeling lost, confused, and overwhelmed is okay. Give yourself permission to experience the full range of emotions that accompany grief. Allow yourself the grace to move through this process at your own pace, trusting that each step brings you closer to adjusting to a new normal and moving forward.

Additionally, emotional reactions may be accompanied by physical ones. Our hearts may race, blood pressure rises, faintness may occur, breathing may be fast, and body temperature may increase or decrease.

This behavior does not take the time to evaluate what the best response could be at the moment"; it reacts as when falling, and you automatically react to brace your landing.

How can you help?

Remember, when a loss is experienced, each person's reaction is specific to them and their situation. Don't compare! Don't judge. A reaction will happen, and it is okay.

Be empathetic. Understand a reaction was not planned.

Reflecting on Grief

Grief usually provides a space to reflect on the loss. Reflection is a powerful tool that allows us to think deeply or carefully about it. As the reality of the situation begins to seep in, there's an internal struggle to reconcile the 'before' and 'after.' The mind revisits shared moments, dissects words exchanged, and dances intricately between the past and the present. Every memory is magnified; every interaction is scrutinized.

We look at the loss as if looking in a mirror. We stare at the aerial view of the loss and then begin to dissect it into individual pieces to gain a more detailed overall picture.

The recent conversation with the doctor when our health issue was addressed is amplified. The words from our employer, "We are downsizing and your job has been eliminated," are flashing in our head. The relationship that just ended has left a myriad of questions in your mind. Whatever the loss, grief invites you to reflect on it.

The loss experienced shows up and beckons you to review its details as if reading the fine print on a contract you are about to sign.

For many months after my father died, I got up in the morning and felt like I was staring in the mirror at the details of his hospitalization and eventual death. It became an "instant replay"; I remembered the meticulous details of experiencing his stroke, his fall in the hospital, his decline in health, and his eventual death.

Allow someone grieving the opportunity to reflect. It is normal to revisit thoughts, situations, and conversations. The mind takes the loss like throwing a pebble in a pond, and each ripple connects to a thought, emotion, or experience about the circumstance.

This behavior likes to do a rewind and replay. Often, a person will repeat this process in their mind over and over again. Many have stated they were hoping something changed where the loss didn't happen or didn't negatively affect them, or they misinterpreted how it was communicated.

Reflecting on the loss is a meaningful and healthy part of engaging with grief.

How can you help?

Grievers want to be listened to. I learned with the Grief Recovery Method we need to be a "heart with ears."

Thank the griever for sharing their heart with you. Avoid telling a "grief story" of your own. Do not tell someone, "I know how you feel." If the loss is a death, avoid phrases – they are in a better place – at least you enjoyed them for "X" years – you have to be strong.

Look for ways to help and support the person grieving; do not say, "If you need anything, just let me know."

Rethinking Grief

Grief knows how to be polite and allows you a vacuum to rethink everything. Rethinking is not reflecting; reflecting is reseeding what happened. As we rethink, this is where we begin to entertain the "what if," "I should have," "I wish," "I didn't think this would happen," and numerous other phrases.

This behavior can cause our minds to race, striving to recreate what we would like the situation to be like. Rethinking can tend to leave you with many scenarios that you envisioned would happen yet never will.

Clients I have worked with routinely revisit rethinking their grief journey. They grasp for a different reality that can never be and hope for a different outcome that will never occur. Rethinking, for many, enables them to reshape the past momentarily until reality knocks on the door of their mind.

One griever repeatedly stated, "If I had been there, this would have been different, she would have not gotten in that accident that changed her life." This father was taking on some of the blame for the outcome of the accident because he was not present when it happened. Grief has a way of causing you to wear guilt that was not designed for you to put on.

The majority of grievers are going to have this behavior reintroduce itself throughout the grieving process. They have to recognize continuing to step back into the past is not going to help support them moving forward and adjusting to a new normal.

How can you help?

Be empathetic; this behavior can cause the mind to be at war. Gently guide the person back to the present, the now. Rethinking does not change the past or predict the future. Encourage reflecting on joyful memories and times. If the griever appears stuck and experiencing negative emotions hindering them moving forward, suggest professional help from a therapist or grief coach.

Refreshing Through Grief

Grief has a way of engulfing your life and becoming an ongoing focus as you attempt to move through your daily activities. It has a way of lurking around, waiting to attach itself to wherever you go in thought or situation. It begins to become engulfing and overwhelming. When we see things transpiring in our lives, our inner self is crying out to be refreshed.

I had a client explain refreshing in such a metaphoric way. She did not even realize she had given me a magnificent picture of one of the behaviors of grief.

She said verbatim: "Imagine a scorching day where the sun beats down without mercy. You are outside, with no shade, dressed in black, so you are drawing more heat. You feel parched and drained. In the midst of this oppressive heat, a cool glass of water appears like a mirage in the desert. Reaching for the glass, you begin to anticipate the first taste of it and your mouth begins to salivate. As you take that first refreshing sip, you can feel the revitalizing power of hydration spreading through your body, quenching your thirst and rejuvenating your senses."

Water is so refreshing to the body. I have developed a habit that when I first wake up in the morning, I drink at least eight ounces of water before I drink anything else. As I drink water, there is an awareness, and I can feel it traveling down my esophagus and venturing off in other directions to lubricate and moisturize my organs.

Just as water is essential for physical well-being, self-care is crucial for emotional and mental wellness, especially during times of grief. When we are grieving, it can be easy to neglect our own needs as we navigate through the pain and sadness of grief and loss. It is precisely during these challenging moments that self-care becomes even more vital.

Refreshing involves doing something welcoming or stimulating to address self-care and offset grieving. This behavior moves the energy and focus from grief to establishing and maintaining a healthy relationship with yourself as you grieve.

In the midst of sorrow, it can be easy to forget the importance of nourishing our bodies and minds. By embracing self-care during grief, we are replenishing our energy and creating space for hope and resilience to bloom within us. Self-care has the power to refresh our spirits and guide us towards a brighter moment.

Appropriate self-care will also encompass addressing your emotional well-being. Our emotions tend to drive our thinking and our behavior, so it is necessary to sift through how we feel and how we think and move our emotions back into a space that is healthy and safe for us.

It's also helpful to cultivate a positive mindset during difficult times. This doesn't mean forcing yourself to be happy all the time but rather shifting your perspective to focus on the things that bring you joy. Gratitude practices, such as keeping a journal of things you are thankful for, can help you appreciate the good things in your life, even amidst grief.

Practicing mindfulness has proven to be a healthy way to promote well-being and emotional balance. Mindfulness helps us stay in the now and the present and increases our focus on what we can do with the "here and now" that is beneficial.

This behavior encourages us to be proactive on our grief journey.

How can you help?

Encourage the griever to focus on themselves by introducing appropriate activities to uplift their mood and spirit. Suggest seeking out a mindfulness practitioner to support their desire to stay present. Partner with someone to create joyful experiences that positively stimulate the mind. Begin an electronic "buddy journal" together to encourage and share thoughts, ideas, gratitude, and praises (sign an agreement of confidentiality and privacy with one another). Have the griever start a private journal for themselves and write in it at least three times a week.

Redirecting Through Grief

Eventually, on your grief journey, you begin to determine how you will get up each day and continue healthily after the loss. Redirecting is the behavior that positively moves you in a positive direction.

Many individuals await "closure," and you often hear the phrase "I just need closure." Closure puts a period at the end of your loss. It has closed the door and implies that you will not go back that way again. By definition, closure is an act or process of closing something.

Let me suggest we identify a need to move forward and put a semicolon after your loss. This continues to connect your loss (the past) with your present (here and now) and creates a bridge to move into tomorrow (your future).

The semicolon allows you to not just stare at the loss; it gives you space to see the entire relationship. Redirecting steers you away from the tunnel vision that can occur when the loss has magnified, and other parts of the relationship have diminished or become hard to find. The semicolon joins two related independent clauses. A semicolon is useful for creating a smooth connection between two interrelated ideas or thoughts instead of using a period, which creates a full stop.

This behavior continually beckons you to walk the path and "adjust to a new normal" after the loss. It wants you to take your memories and emotions on that walk while you travel into a new space with your grief and loss. It's a process; be patient as this redirecting unfolds.

Redirecting may involve taking baby steps, not necessarily a long jump. The goal is to move forward healthily and appropriately.

Your life seemed to be mapped out a certain way. A loss occurred, and your whole direction with your emotions, thinking, and future changes. It is like getting directions from your GPS to go to a location and unintentionally straying from the course of travel it suggested. Your GPS immediately states, "recalculating route." As you redirect, you have to recalculate your route. You are adjusting to a new normal.

This behavior does not have a timeline and will not appear in a queue that indicates "let's do it now."

How can you help?

Observe the grieving person as you see them headed in a positive new direction. Provide the needed support to help them along the way. This is also a great time to be a good listener, but not necessarily a time for your suggestions. Be present and willing to embark on the redirected journey with them.

Summarizing the Behaviors of Grief

The behaviors of grief are not linear. They will not unfold in a systematic way that allows you to anticipate what will happen next. Keep in mind that grief is unique to everyone's life, so the behaviors, while consistent with grievers, will appear in different ways.

Initially, Reacting to Grief is the first behavior to be seen. From there, each behavior appears in the griever's journey based on its individual circumstances.

For information on coaching, workshops, training or speaking:

To Contact Jan:

Growing Through My Journey

Phone:317/647-6645

Email: jan@jandavidson.org

Website: htttps://www.jandavidson.org/

Instagram: https://www.instagram.com/growingthroughmyjourney/

LinkedIn: https://www.linkedin.com/in/jan-davidson-she-her-yeye-89206513/

LS Kirkpatrick

LS Kirkpatrick, publisher of writers2readers, LLC, is the dynamo podcast host of the Value In You show and an Award winning multiple International #1 Best-selling Author, Award winning International Speaker, Guiding Life Coach, loving wife, caring mother of 4, and energetic MeeMah to 15 grandchildren. She was encouraged by her children to publish the books she had specifically written for her grandchildren and in less than ten months, LS wrote and published eleven books, eight reaching international #1 best-seller status. And now she helps others write their story and become published authors. LS is in the process of organizing and creating the Orphans & Widows, a non-profit charitable organization; raising funds for organizations who take care of the needs of orphaned or wayward children and the newly widowed. As a Guiding Life Coach, for women ages 40-65, she guides you to "See the value in yourself and live your purpose with courage". LS loves what she does, working with you to achieve your dreams. Her golden nugget for you is "You have great value, You are worthy, You are enough, and You definitely matter".

Phenomenal Me!

By LS Kirkpatrick

If you had met me two and a half years ago, you would have called me a good neighbor and a nice person, which is excellent, by the way, but that was it.

I had no purpose in life. Don't get me wrong, I loved my family and was a doting grandmother, but aside from them, there wasn't much more about me. Well, hold your horses right here because that is only a message I played in my head time and time again. It was not the truth for me, and it certainly is not the truth for you.

How do I know this? Easy answer. I discovered a secret that was right in front of me the whole time. I am valuable, I am worthy, I am enough, and I matter. This is true for you, too. This discovery came shortly after I began my journey as an author. Here is a little insight into why I even stepped into this journey.

I had spent my life raising my children, working when times were tough, and still being a woman who enjoyed life. I had spent over forty years doing genealogy for our own family and the families of others, even helping Daughters of the American Revolutionary War find their patriots for membership. I loved it but couldn't seem to make business out of it. I had absolutely no business sense. I had never been around anyone with their own business, not to where I could learn from them. There were a couple of tactics that I thought were not ways that I wanted to do business. So, I let it go.

I went back to college and earned my A.S. and A.A.S. degrees at 58 years of age. Then, my mom had multiple strokes, and I chose to stay home and take care of her. Life happens, and the choices we make are our choices. I longed to do something positive with my life, and I was learning to count my days. I was not in my 20s anymore. I know we never know when our time on earth is done, but as I was (am) getting older, I wondered, "Is this all I was ever going to do with my life? Did I not have an even better legacy to leave my grandchildren with"?

I loved telling my grandchildren stories. There is nothing like the looks on their faces, the exclamations and giggles during the tale-

and then, one day, we moved out of state for my husband's work. It was more challenging to tell them stories over the phone and try to remember what we talked about (with fifteen grandchildren in 5 different homes, you might understand why!)

I decided to write their stories on paper and send them in the mail. Then I put them in books you can order online, one copy for them and one for me so that we could read together. The more I wrote, the more the stories progressed with illustrations or photos, and in one story I wrote, I asked a young friend of mine to do the illustrations. She is a fantastic artist, and that is when my daughter told me, "Mom, you have to publish this book for others." I said, "Who would want this? It was made just for your girls". Well, after three years of convincing me, I took the step to write some other stories and put them on Amazon, and nothing happened, no crickets, not even gathering dust.

Then I saw an ad on YouTube for a course to get your books out of the cricket zone and into the selling zone and how to run a business. At this time, my husband had been home for one year, going on two years, from a work injury, and things were beyond tight. The course was free, so I said yes and took the leap of faith to take that one step toward my vision of success. A whole new world opened up to me. To make a long story shorter, I had eleven books printed and published in ten months, and I was now an eight-time International #1 Bestselling Author.

I learned how to publish my books, find illustrators, cover artists, and editors, and market my books. I became a podcast host and now host my weekly International live show. I have made some of the most wonderful friends and colleagues - even ones who are not authors! We support each other to grow in what we do and be there through all the ups and downs, and there can be many.

Now, you might be super happy for me, or you might be saying, "Yeah! For you, but what's this got to do with me?" I am so glad you asked that! It means that you, too, can take one step forward into the purpose you know you were meant to be in.

You don't know what your purpose is? Well, what really makes you come alive? That is what others need! Don't know how to even start? Find someone who is successful at what you want to do, learn from them, and then pour yourself into it. It doesn't matter if there are 100 others out there doing what you do because you are you, and they won't be able to do what you do or how you do it. You are unique. I know this because no one else has had to make the choices you have had to make, act, or react to the choices that others have made that directly affected you, and no one will in the future. This makes you so very valuable and gives you a unique perspective that no one else has! That is where your value comes from, which makes you worthy, not what you do or who people say you are. That value and worth is what makes you enough, which is why you matter!

Yes, that may seem simple, but usually it is simple. It takes you telling yourself that it won't happen if you don't do it. There are some strategies that I have learned to help me keep moving forward no matter how hard it is, even when I want to quit.

Here are the *seven strategies* to help guide you for now:

Strategy 1: Mindset

This was a new concept to me. I didn't even know what it meant. I had to learn that my subconscious mind dominated my conscious mind. So, even if my conscious mind was saying good job, the more significant, more obnoxious subconscious mind was saying, "Yeah, and you will fail at it like you did everything else in your past." But I had a new weapon to deflect that. I learned how to take each thought captive. I heard the negative talk, captured it, and said, "You don't live here anymore. I have a new, powerful, positive thought, so go on and get outta here!". And you know what? It came back, but I told it again, and eventually, I realized it was not coming back! I had to do this with several negative thoughts.

Strategy 2: Affirmations

I hadn't even heard of the word, but I guessed what it meant. I barely touched the surface of what it meant. Daily, I write down three affirmations and read out 150 other affirmations. Why? By saying them out loud, the daily affirmations become my new subconscious, and when something good happens, my whole brain rejoices; when that happens, I feel better and energized and can keep going. When something negative happens, I pause long enough to learn from it, why it didn't work, and then move on with this newly discovered information. If you do not have daily affirmations, your brain will freak out when a negative happens, and you will get stuck for a time. That is no fun.

Strategy 3: Your Top People

Surround yourself with people who uplift you, encourage you, and are there for you in the down days. Why? If you only have people around you who are negative and doubtful, you will be, too. Who you spend your most time with are those who influence you the most. So, why not be influenced the most by those who are uplifting and encouraging to you?

Don't feel bad if your family is not your top people. They may have your best in mind, but family cannot always see the vision that you see. That doesn't mean getting rid of them; it means that perhaps it is time to spend more of your time with others helping you reach your vision.

Strategy 4: Journal

Journaling is not for everyone, but it can help so much. Even if you are not consistently journaling, you can still journal. What journaling does at night is to help you sort out the day, and it gives you a place to put the things to rest that would keep you awake. You are not getting rid of them; they will be there in the morning, but you now have set them aside so you and your brain can rest well for the night. In the morning, you can write down any epiphanies you wake up with and organize your day.

Yes, I wrote my journal to ask the questions I need to ask myself daily to sort and prepare. I have a daily calendar set up every half hour to help prepare for all that happens in a day. I used to do it every 15 minutes, then I realized I could accomplish the same with every half hour, and it uses less paper, making for a lighter book.

This particular journal also helps me set up goals the right way. I had no idea the impact they would make, and it reminds me to take a day off just for me and/or my family, with backed-up support on why it is crucial.

Whichever journal you use, use one. Remember, if you skip a few days, journal what went on when you return.

Strategy 5: Don't Quit

You may think that is a "no-brainer," but this is why people's dreams die with them in the cemetery. Besides the fear of "what if," quitting is the number two reason many people don't achieve their dreams. It is really tough at times to pursue your dreams. If it is consistently tough, talk to someone who has achieved their dream and ask for guidance. Yes, you will have a few times (okay, I had several times) when I wanted to quit, but I stopped, paused, and reevaluated), which brings us to the next strategy.

Strategy 6: The Importance of the Pause

I once visited with an older gentleman who was further ahead of me but had yet to quite reach his vision of success, though he seemed to be doing very well at getting there. When I told him my vision, he laughed at me and told me to be realistic, that I was too old to reach such a lofty dream. We ended our conversation cordially, and I crossed him off the list of those from whom I would seek guidance.

What was he talking about? He could only see his vision as far as his limiting beliefs would let him. Therefore, he thought I would never be able to reach mine. If I had listened to him, I would not be where I am today or where I am going to be tomorrow.

He also told me that I should never take a pause. Anyone who takes a pause is actually quitting and starts over each time. This is NOT true. A pause is a necessary part of your journey! When you pause, you are reevaluating if this is the right path or if you have gone down a rabbit hole (a never-ending road to nowhere). Are you on a detour or a distraction? Is there something more you can do, or are you doing too much?

The pause is so important to keep you advancing into your success. Everyone has a different vision of what success means to them. No one can tell you your vision; only you can do that. They can guide you or block you. You decide who to listen to and what to listen to.

Strategy 7: Last but not least and not the final one, you can find more for you

C E L E B R A T E, *Celebrate*!

I lost a client today! Hooray! Because I learned so much about what people want and what they are looking for, the next time, I will win!

I woke up today, and I am alive!

There was hot coffee!

The plumbing is working!

Celebrate even the little things. My pen didn't run out of ink in the middle of a training. Whatever you can find to celebrate, do it.

Celebrate the big things! I got a new client today! I sold out of my books! I sold a book! I got that contract I've been working on for seven months.

Celebrate the in-between things! I was on time for all of my meetings today. I wrote in my journal three days in a row. I had a negative thought; I captured it and cast it to the curb.

The purpose of celebrating is to energize and ignite your brain. Once it gets one celebration, it wants more and more, and you will find more ways to be victorious. More ways to conquer. More ways to succeed in achieving your vision of success.

You can use these strategies for your life as well. Take care of yourself. Be kind to yourself. Celebrate yourself. Look at yourself in the mirror and tell yourself how great you are! Reject any negative thoughts that you might want to whisper in your ear. You are valuable. You are worthy. You are enough. You matter.

Today, I am writing books, which I love to do, especially anthologies. I have one that is all about giving; that is why it is called The Giving Book, and it's in its 4th volume! I am in negotiations for a non-profit for raising funds for nonprofits that support widows and the orphaned (and homeless) children. I have a community that is thriving, and there's my podcast that has turned into a show. I am speaking and writing for others. As each task is completed, I'm already moving forward with the next one.

Grow, learn, serve others, and repeat, and repeat. It is an exciting future! You don't have to do what I do, you shouldn't do what I do, you should do what you want to do. Do it well, and don't give up because there are times when it will be tough but keep going. Pause to see where you are, if it is the direction you want to go, and if what you are doing is getting you there. Get out of the safety and comfort of the usual and step forward into your purpose. You matter.

To connect with LS: https://www.LSKirkpatrick.com

Natasha Davini

I'm Natasha Davini, and I was raised on the tough streets of Columbus, Ohio. I'm the eldest of three siblings and now a proud mother of seven children myself. Due to my mother having me at a young age, I grew up in the presence of my grandparents. I was the peculiar kid who never quite found their place. I've always had a strong desire to learn, which resulted in me receiving multiple awards during my academic journey. Due to being ostracized by family and peers, I have developed kindness, understanding, and empathy. I successfully navigated my way out of poverty, near-death encounters, and dubious situations during my youth. Adversity couldn't deter me from seeking my personal definition of success. In 2014, I proudly graduated with my RN license and became a lifetime member of the National Society of Collegiate Scholars. Despite that, life had alternative plans because I was harboring a secret that would ultimately unlock my path to success. You see, I possess the incredible talent of connecting the living and the deceased as a medium. I consider my biggest achievement to be collaborating with law enforcement agencies, missing persons, organizations, and families in search of answers. By stepping out of the shadows, I empower those who can no longer speak, bringing closure to grieving families and resolving unanswered questions.

Igniting your inner Phoenix.

By Natasha Davini, ND.

As children, we never expected the trials, heartbreak, and tragedies that would come with adulthood. Our world was brimming with fairy tales, magic, and uncharted adventures. They advised us to dream big but with a realistic perspective, as it could often be unattainable. As kids, we inhabited a world that frequently defied logical comprehension. Did you have any specific career goals as a child? Who were you prior to being influenced by societal conditioning and expectations? Who were you back when imagination and enchantment held a powerful presence in your thoughts? Consider the idea that the very magic you felt as a child could be the secret to your success.

Did you experience any inexplicable events during your childhood? Were you plagued by a creepy feeling that engulfed us as we detected something amiss in a house? Do you know the feeling of waking up from a dream so realistic that it sends shivers down your spine? There are occurrences in life that defy logical explanations, yet we dismiss them as mere coincidences or figments of imagination. Let's entertain the idea that it's not just imagination. What if our truest authenticity allows our minds to possess limitless capabilities?

In my childhood, I had the unique ability to interact with spirits that no one else could perceive. In my earliest memories, I recall engaging in conversations with imaginary friends. Yet, these companions would intricately narrate the circumstances leading to their deaths, going as far as showing me visual glimpses of the incidents. During my childhood, I would enthusiastically share my observations, experiences, and what I heard with anyone willing to listen. It never crossed my mind that people would question me or be afraid of the unknown.

My grandmother would reassure me it was only my imagination and that she, too, would imagine people who weren't really there when she was a little girl. "It was normal for a creative mind," she'd proclaim. She promised me that as I grew older, my imagination would fade, and I wouldn't see them anymore. Still, my imagination carried on from my childhood all the way into my adult years. Every individual I encountered had a companion that only I could perceive. Hospitals, oh no, they were everywhere! Interestingly, I discovered cemeteries were consistently the most serene and hushed environments for both me and the individuals interred there. They would always entrust me with messages to deliver to the people they were with or intended for.

One of my most memorable experiences was playing tea party with a lady wearing a pink dress. My mom specifically told me not to share this information with others because she believed they wouldn't be able to comprehend it. One day, we were going through a family picture album, and I shrieked with excitement, "That's the lady mama!!" My mama turned pale as she stated, that's your granny Kairis. She passed away months after my birth. In hindsight, my mother's intention was to shield me from the life that awaited me.

Because I was different, my family targeted me, my friends could not play with me, and others feared me. They ridiculed me, ostracized me, and even made me believe I was Satan himself. As I reached adulthood, I hid who I was because of fear of once again being subjected to limited minds with limited beliefs. For years, I diminished myself to satisfy those without knowledge or self-acceptance. Unfortunately, I, like many in my family, succumbed to the soul trap of generational trauma, habits, and codependency.

Amidst my quest for acceptance, I faced many circumstances that, thanks to God's grace, I overcame, leading me to where I am now. I became a mother at just 16 years old. As a young mother with limited education, I choose a path of alcohol, drugs, and fast money. With a fake ID in hand, I walked into the nightclub, auditioned, and got hired. That rabbit hole introduced me to situations I had only ever seen in movies, and now they've become my reality. One night, in particular, the whole day felt off. I left the club that night and suddenly found myself with a broken jaw, trapped in a trunk while duct-taped. I just had become the victim of a pimp.

Thankfully, I was a quick thinker and calculated my escape. Armed with my abilities and seeking someone to trust, I looked for a "John" in Las Vegas, Nevada, to aid me in getting back home. There was an older man sitting at the blackjack table, and I'll never forget his face.

Once we were alone, I explained everything to him, and he wasted no time getting me on the next Greyhound bus back home. I successfully conquered the nightmares that tormented me for years with the help of therapy. Therapy allowed me to reclaim my power, sobriety, and wholeness once more. Ever since that moment, I have resolved to make something meaningful out of my life.

Moving forward, I obtained my GED while taking care of two children. I left the stripping industry and started working as a waitress. After years of dedication, I achieved my goal of becoming a manager at the beloved Waffle House. Regardless of favorable conditions, including decent pay, I had to fight for acceptance from my peers and family. Regardless of pretending to be normal by their definition, my presence would trigger those around me. It goes without saying that I continued to scare people until that very day. I held onto the belief for years that one morning, I would wake up and be just like everyone else, but my waiting was futile.

Despite my efforts, my family still considered me an outcast and treated me differently. I was coerced into a box and manipulated to think there was something wrong with me. Religion replaced alcohol as my means to free myself from those demons. I strived to prove myself by living a normal life, including getting my RN license, obtaining a naturopathic doctorate, buying a home, and raising a family. My conviction was that once I proved my normalcy, they would accept me. However, this would soon prove to all be in vain.

The greater my accomplishments, the more I became a target for criticism from those close to me. The realization was that jealousy, resentment, and fear don't dissipate just because one adheres to another's perception of life. If anything, it exacerbated the abuse because individuals with insecurities are more likely to feel their failures amplified by the accomplishments of others. This marked the beginning of being crucified, with slander, drama, and fights occurring in rooms where I wasn't present. Despite separating myself years ago, they always seemed to come knocking on my door metaphorically. It had become apparent their fears had imprisoned my life's trajectory.

Fear had kept me bound in an endless cycle of self-doubt and limitations. My life turned into a prison of stagnation, self-sabotage, and people-pleasing by surrounding myself with those who had limited mindsets and beliefs. It was only when I began observing the chains I had put on myself that I could let go of fear and financial burdens and fully embrace my highest potential. I discovered triumph in the midst of tragedy. All upon stepping with faith and allowing myself the safety net of authenticity.

Even with all the naysayers, I never stopped believing in myself, and I was determined to achieve success, whatever that meant for me! I, like most people, suffered the significant loss of my cousin, best friend, and biggest fan in 2019, which set the trajectory for the woman I am today. This also followed a devastating diagnosis of Systemic lupus with kidney failure that was triggered at the expense of a narcissist, where I lost everything. I had to examine my soul, alter my way of thinking, and embrace my true identity! To honor her memory, I emerged from obscurity and revealed my abilities as a medium to the world.

The pain I experienced rapidly turned into my driving force. Lindsay never showed any fear towards me and persistently begged me for years to share my gift with the world. In my journey of self-discovery, I came to understand that fear is merely an illusion. Being a medium, I've always known that death is not the finality for us. It was simply an energy conversion. The moment had come for me to change my mindset, life, and energy. I had lived my life based on another's perception of who I should be to appease their sense of comfort. It was now time to emerge as the bridge that would link the living and deceased.

When I dared to ask the challenging questions most shy away from, I uncovered my authentic self. I encountered a timid young girl inside who had mistakenly believed that fear was something tangible. I uncovered that she had endured neglect, abuse, premature expectations, and rejection of her true identity. Fear, loneliness, and powerlessness overwhelmed her. Society's conditioning of children to conform instead of embracing their authenticity leads to the loss of their creativity and unique spark. By asking those questions and addressing the reality of the situation, I ignited my inner Phoenix, one spark at a time!

I let my true self shine, allowing my inner child to speak freely. The magic of fearlessness unveiled my purpose to me. I served as a therapist for both the living and the deceased, tasked with connecting realms unseen by many. Few possessed the gift of my uniqueness, which could alleviate the suffering of many. My authenticity became my success. I found success by defying society's expectations of normality! Success became normal once I stopped prioritizing others' opinions, which fuels fear or insecurities.

Our beliefs define our limitations about ourselves and those in our vicinity. One's perception of self can either create a symphony of success or blind one's visions, dreams, and aspirations. We have the option to either persist with the same actions and hope for tangible outcomes or systematically modify one factor at a time to bring our dreams to fruition. To reset one's life, one must reconnect with the magical essence experienced in childhood. When we are young, we fear nothing and live without regret, immersed in imagination and enchantment.

Instead of fear, we embraced trust in the outcome. Failure taught us it's just another step towards success. Falling off our bikes didn't deter us from trying again. We rose, tended to our wounds, and swiftly resumed our ride. We would ride that bike nonstop, from morning to evening, or until it couldn't go any further! We didn't allow anyone to impede our success or doubt our abilities. Children, even amid fear, do it anyway because they know eventually they'll have success.

When I immersed myself in the magic of childhood again, I understood that there were no limits. I see magic in all that surrounds me, from the graceful birds soaring during sunsets to raindrops creating a sweet melody on rooftops during summer storms. As we grow older, the search for magic often fades, and life loses its allure. We fall into monotonous routines and crave validation from fellow adults.

Becoming rich, famous, or being part of the latest trend is what many associate with success. Society instructs us that material possessions primarily measure one's success. Nevertheless, none of us will take any of this along. You'll always experience a sense of dissatisfaction if you're constantly chasing the next big thing or conforming to someone else's notion of success. Will you forever pursue happiness, only to question why it remains elusive?

Most people become distracted or lose sight of who they are, even though we all have a purpose in this lifetime. They obsess over discovering the purpose they seek, unaware their protective armor conceals it. Conditioning, self-discovery deficiency, and the desire for approval led to the activation of the armor. I could only achieve success by unleashing my eccentric abilities after shedding burdens that were not truly mine. By questioning my identity in contrast to societal expectations, my life underwent a transformative journey akin to a Phoenix's rebirth.

My success became tangible once I left the rat race of conformity. I wholeheartedly embraced my uniqueness and let everyone know I am a medium without fear or persecution. I overcame the fear of others' opinions about me. I cut out those who were stuck in narrow mindsets and beliefs from my life and emerged as a Phoenix from the ashes for all to see. Removed the mask of self-doubt and chose to place my trust in myself and my abilities. It occurred to me that true success begins with our own perception.

We must formulate a plot of trusting ourselves while activating fearlessness to begin a harvest of successful endeavors. Success means many things to many types of people. It's all about exploring oneself to determine what success looks like for them. It's a process of observation, elimination, and preservation. We must observe our behaviors and beliefs to either eliminate what they taught us to be versus preservation of who we aspire to be.

By adapting or reactivating the magical fearlessness we had as children, it becomes easier to dig layer by layer to eliminate people-pleasing behaviors. We learn to trust ourselves and our abilities to succeed. We no longer seek approval from outside influence but seek validation of fulfillment to self-serving prophecy healthily. Excellence is the reflection captured in the soul's mirror. It becomes the foundation of accomplishment and acknowledgment of the most authentic version of self. Authenticity, as the glue, will stabilize one's mindset, fuel their determination, and push past limits they wouldn't have otherwise achieved!

Remaining true to ourselves keeps us in a perpetual state of happiness and bliss. Take a minute, pause and reflect. What is my personal definition of happiness? Additionally, are we remaining true to ourselves as we seek happiness or success? Have we relied on the perceptions and expectations of others to guide our journey to success? Many people prioritize acceptance over happiness, hindering them from achieving their goals, dreams, or personal success. They enable themselves to seek a societal definition of success versus the root of success, happiness.

The moment we realize conformity hinders our progress, we can start making a difference. It all begins when we no longer feel the need to apologize for not conforming to society's standards. Once again, question whether you're prepared to reveal your true individuality over acceptance. Now is the time to seek the magic of being true to yourself rather than seeking society's approval and discovering what success truly means for you.

By embracing our true selves without remorse, we can heal both ourselves and the inherited trauma. When we discard doubts, fears, and self-imposed limitations, we enter a realm of unwavering confidence where success is inevitable. Success becomes attainable when we break free from the expectations others place on us. By embracing the childlike energy of magic and wonder, we can discover happiness everywhere. The liberation felt from exiting being accepted to our authentic version of self is unfathomably regenerating.

It reignites the regeneration of our minds to focus on solutions versus everyday problems. It's okay that not every day is filled with happiness. The page may not always turn as quickly as we'd like, but ultimately, we are the author of our own chapter. Instead of fixating on the dark clouds, direct your focus toward the blossoming flowers in the midst of the storm. The sun continues to shine, even if we don't see it right away amidst passing storms. In childhood, we sought to jump in the puddles versus hide from the thunder.

The remnants of burnt debris have given rise to some of the most breathtaking things in the world. Don't let a handful of embers prevent you from reaching your desired goals. Peel back the layers of your being to reveal the unique meaning of success. Show up each day as the truest version of yourself, unapologetically! Allow fearlessness to guide your every step, and find joy in even the smallest successes. By examining the true meaning of success beyond appeasing others and ego, the answers will become evident.

By embodying our true essence, we move forward with wisdom, determination, and grace. The façade is done, so we don't have to play the game of charades anymore. Putting on a show is no longer necessary to obtain acceptance. There's no longer any reason to compete because the only competition we see is our own reflection gazing back upon us every morning.

The awe of life will be rediscovered. Authentic connections will develop, and achievement is reliant on personal growth. The recognition of the self in the mirror comes from the significance regained by small things. The soul's rhythm will revive childhood from being a mere pastime. Accompanied by a profound sense of gratitude for life, the eyes will regain confidence and radiance.

Having self-trust is crucial for any endeavor we face. There's no more doubt or hesitation about our capabilities or reaching our destination. Success fills us with a surreal and unfathomable feeling. When we opt for authenticity, we instinctively rely on our abilities to make wise choices. Once we have this mastered, our purpose becomes apparent.

First, we must take part in introspection. Upon self-reflection, what does personal success look like to me? What prevents us from embracing the journey of self-discovery? Does the fear of not being capable enough hinder our ability to achieve our goals, dreams, and aspirations? Does success hold the highest priority in my life? How do our individual fears hinder us from living authentically?

The process commences with confirming your identity. It all begins when one embraces their true essence, disregarding the societal constructs imposed upon us. Upon abandoning our shield of protection, we come to understand its irrelevance to our fulfillment. The moment has come. Trust yourself completely and live a life free from fear, doubt, and uncertainty. Once we stop diluting ourselves to avoid intimidating others, that's when our lives truly start.

My success became imminent when I made the choice to live authentically, no matter who fears me. Despite many challenges and hardships, I persevered to share this testimony. I transformed my fears into resilience and liberated myself from seeking validation. I made my proclamation by eliminating all other options. Being unwaveringly authentic is all you need. Avoid restricting your capabilities based on biased minds that cannot explore themselves. To find the key to success, show up daily with determination, vision, and unapologetically be yourself.

**

To contact Natasha:

thephoenixcode616.org

NatashaDavini@outlook.com

(614) 817-4305

Sandra Saenz

Sandra Saenz is CEO of Dream Team Communications, LLC., supporting corporations and individuals in 32 countries in 3 languages for 30 years. She is internationally known as a Mindset Mastery Expert and Global Leadership Speaker and Coach. She lived in Europe for 20 years and has produced long-term Leadership Academies and personal development programs, which are still ongoing all over the world. "Helping people connect with their magnificence." is her mission statement. As a **Certified Dale Carnegie Trainer** and member of the prestigious Global Trainer Team, she was named Top Business Trainer for 4 consecutive years in Vienna, Austria. (First American to get licensed in Vienna.) Sandra is Texas born, a published author and former advertising executive, supervising 8 countries in the CEE region for Ogilvy & Mather Worldwide Communications. She has conducted training for General Motors in Moscow; Leadership programs for Fortune 500 companies in Denmark, Rio de Janeiro, Oxfordshire, Madrid, Amsterdam, Chile and Senegal, Africa among many others.

Certifications:

5 Dale Carnegie Licenses: Leadership, Personal Development, High Impact Presentations, Sales Training and Curriculum Design. Vitale Awakened Millionaire Academy, Certified Manifestation Energetics Coach, EFT Tapping

BMW, IBM, General Motors, AT&T, Adidas, Procter & Gamble, American Express, Maersk Shipping, Kraft Foods

Books/Publications: Bring Your "A" Game, What Channel Are You On? Take Back Your Power

Stay YOU: Live from Your Point of Power

The Change [21]

Sandra lives in San Diego, California, loves the beach, singing in choir, baseball games and travel.

Streaming the Supernatural: Your Birthright
"Listening is a talent. Streaming your source is a superpower."

By Sandra Saenz

Waiting is painful for us! The latest stats show that most people do not want to wait more than 4 minutes in line for a purchase. We definitely do not like to wait. In our current world, waiting implies "not living" between activities that matter. That concept is crucial. Think about it: when waiting, we feel like we are "not living." Wow. That's why we have a culture of streaming. We like streaming a movie online because it's available to us at our command, exactly when we want it, right? We decide where and when. Well, what if you could have, at your command, any answer to a question or confirmation on a hunch or the solution to destroy a panicking fear? In the following few pages, I will share with you how to stream this supernatural source and examples of how I did it to create a successful lifestyle where I can finally stop and tune into true contentment, take time off work, travel, and have "me time" anywhere I wish. In discovering these techniques and case studies, you may also recognize that you may have "streamed the supernatural" without really knowing it!

Moments of Impact

Have you ever had a moment in your life when you took a step towards something, and it seemed against all odds? You made a decision that didn't seem logical, and most people around you seemed surprised and against it. A step that just didn't seem ordinary for you. I call these "Moments of Impact". These moments create a massive shift in the direction of our lives. Besides my story of impact below, a perfect example of a Moment of Impact that changed someone's direction is from the movie Adjustment Bureau, when Matt Damon falls in love the moment he sees Emily Blunt in her ballet solo, and he connects to her sheer love. He has a Moment of Impact that changes his trajectory forever. My Moment caused quite a stir in my family and changed my trajectory, too.

"What are you going to eat in Budapest?"

That was the first question a family member asked when I announced that I was moving to Budapest, Hungary, on my own, for a fixed-term marketing contract. This was the first barrage of interrogations:

"Why would you move to a country where you don't know anybody?"

"What language do they speak there?"

"Why in the world, would you leave a good paying, stable job and great house?"

I was a 32-year-old Texas girl, a year after a 'wake-up" call divorce and on my way to becoming a full-fledged workaholic. My Texas family and work colleagues were confused and against my relocation to Hungary, a small country they knew very little about. I remember feeling betrayed by their reactions and surprised at the fears that surfaced. I was so ready and excited to embark on my new venture. This was the FIRST TIME I realized that I was streaming the supernatural... without really knowing it.

I had traveled to Budapest on business. During one of my trips, as I was having dinner overlooking the Danube, my client turned to me and asked, "You always say you love it here, why don't you just move here?" I was speechless and just sat there, taking in the provocative question. He then proceeded and said, "I can give you subcontract work for 3 to 6 months and then you can decide how you like it." I said YES. Within 10 minutes, we discussed terms and projects. I remember feeling excited, eager, and curious all at the same time. The prospect of this new adventure erased any logic or fear. At that time, I had my dream job with plenty of freedom and variety, a good salary, a house, and my long-awaited Black BMW convertible. But the thought of living in a new European city was too delicious for me to pass up. I got back home and immediately started planning my move. As mentioned earlier, my family and work friends thought I was nuts. I had finally achieved the lifestyle I had planned for, and now I was turning it all upside down by moving to a country most of them had never been to, where I didn't speak the language and was on the other side of the world.

My feelings when I visualized living in Europe and working with new clients who were requesting and ready for my services far outweighed anybody else's doubts or fears. I remember feeling 100% certain that this was my destiny and that I should go. I was STREAMING THE SUPERNATURAL, my source—a birthright we all have.

As it turns out, those six months turned into 18 years, 32 countries, and a new life direction, enriching my life in ways I had never imagined. And I have a pretty big Texas-size imagination! This new life path included teaching and speaking in places from Rio de Janeiro to Vienna to Singapore! I went from being an advertising business executive from Texas to a Global Expert in Leadership and Self-development. This was never my plan. This new life path is much larger and feels like it's part of a bigger picture, a bigger purpose. I feel more connected to everything and everyone. I do things now more "on purpose" than ever before. It's like sailing on a gorgeous ship flowing with the water. The earth is housing the water. The water is supporting the ship, and the ship is carrying me. We are all in collaboration. There is a constant connection available for me. I am never alone.

This new expansive purpose-filled direction may never have come about if I had not said YES to the question, "Why don't you just move here?" This was a huge Moment of Impact on my life. I had no doubt, no hesitation, and no fear. As I write this, I must admit how funny it is that I remember it so clearly after more than three decades. There was a sensation in the center of my lower chest. It felt like something softly fluttering as if waking up after being asleep. I felt strong and unshakeable. Among all the naysayers and fear-based opinions, I was streaming the supernatural. I was streaming my source. . . where all my answers and dreams were living.

Streaming the Supernatural

Let's look at what Streaming the Supernatural really means.

- Streaming - receiving a steady, continuous flow of data available to you at any time and at your convenience.
- Supernatural - beyond earthly, nonrational, unbelievable, and even magical, miraculous, or fabulous.

Streaming the Supernatural involves receiving a steady flow of data that can seem inexplicable, and sometimes miraculous and beyond earthly logic. We can also refer to this steady flow of data or information as intuition, inner guidance, a gut feeling, or listening to your source. Most of us have such busy, full lives that we actually miss the transmission!

This continuous stream of guidance is always there for us. When we are amid decisions, problems, changes, or any other life transitions, the answers to our burning questions already exist in this stream. You can plug into this flow of universal consciousness and STREAM 24/7. Actually, this source of knowledge is omnipresent, always present, and available for us to access anytime. It's like gravity; it's existent whether we use it or not. This Universal stream of source is "for" you. So when you're going through a challenging time or transition, remember the Universe is conspiring "for" you and your highest good. Sometimes, you may realize the reasons why things happened, and other times, you won't know until much later. But rest assured, you are part of this flow of universal source, this stream of consciousness. Whatever you wish to call it: Source, The Universe, God, Faith, Divine Guidance, Your Inner Voice, etc. Just know that it is always there to serve and guide you.

Why Is It Important To Acknowledge The Stream?

Life gets easier.

The more often you acknowledge it, the easier it will be to align with the flow. You will actually move forward with less effort. Information you need or people who can help you will come into your trajectory without you having to work so hard, and you'll be living life more in your sweet spot. More success with less effort.

You will not limit the outcome.

You may also find that when you are plugged into the stream of source, your outcomes will be better and more prominent. You will not limit the outcome. We tend to limit our dreams based on filters left over from past experiences. "Oh, I could never own a house on that lake, because that costs a million dollars, and I've never made anywhere close to that." Well, after about five months of dreaming of a house on Lake Balaton, about an hour from Budapest, in a beautiful village called Szeplak, an elderly couple had a dispute with their children and decided to sell their corner lot lake house to me. They felt I would appreciate it, fix it, and love it more than the squabbling family. Streaming your source brings all kinds of experiences and goodies with no limitations whatsoever. It's not logical. Who said life was logical? Life is unpredictable, continuous, and in a constant state of dynamic creation. So when something like this happens, it's important to acknowledge it and thank and respect your beautiful unlimited source. Whatever you call it: The Supernatural, Source, God, Universal Consciousness, The Universe, Your Inner Guidance or Intuition, in my experience, it's all the same: always there for you to serve your every need.

You'll be a powerful listener and discover things others don't.

Listening and connecting with our source also trains us to be good listeners versus moving forward on autopilot. We are conditioned early on to follow the rules and have goals in order to gain acceptance. We are trained to follow certain proven societal patterns that will bring success. For the most part, we are not taught or encouraged to create intentional pauses of silence and stillness to listen to our inner guidance. Your divine guidance is constantly communicating with you. Here's the biggest mistake we make. We spend more time taking in additional new information versus just being quiet and listening to our own personal customized guidance. These patterns have been taught since childhood, at home, school, work, and even on TV. We are so busy filling our day with action that we often miss the messages of guidance designed just for us. While having so much data at our fingertips is wonderful, it can also be distracting. In my 30-day RELEASE & RESET program, we dive into this concept and let go of what's no longer serving us on the physical, mental, and energetic levels.

Create new ideas on demand versus more of what others are doing.

The need to ingest more and more information from social media and news is an addiction. This addiction is caused and reinforced by a chemical reaction in the brain. When you see something you like, the brain receives a rush of dopamine and this triggers the brain's reward center. This reward of quick pleasure can be quite addicting. Like the hugely successful Lay's potato chip ad, "Bet you can't eat just one." This information addiction to knowing what everyone else is doing or the latest new quick fix to success can take you on a big, long detour. Creating calm, quiet time and streaming your solutions and ideas is not only much easier and faster but also will provide you with fun and creative solutions. Usually, these solutions are new and unique to your combination of talents and desires. Here's a funny and, at the same time, profound example.

Rubber Chickens In Copenhagen

"You must wear a matching full business suit in black, brown or navy during the trainer testing phase in Copenhagen." This first set of instructions indicated how conservative and particular this Danish client would be. While living in Vienna and conducting Leadership training, I was invited to participate and become certified in a prestigious brand-new Leadership program that we would conduct for Maersk Shipping & Oil, based in Denmark. Those of us who became certified would be flown worldwide to teach the course. There were 10 of us, and I was the only American on the team. Needless to say, when I received the stack of notebooks and literally hundreds of slides and cast studies, which we had to learn and deliver, I was nervous and excited all at the same time. Each trainer would be tested as we individually facilitated a live class of leaders, with 8 HR people in the back of the room with clipboards at the headquarters in Copenhagen. It was becoming clear that this was a serious and difficult certification process for Maersk. The fear showed up.

When there's fear and nerves, tune in.

I kept tuning into myself to ensure I was on the right track. In the past, I've sometimes taken on projects, lured by the sheer challenge of them. This motivation came from my brain, not my heart. I asked myself, "Does this feel right? Am I enjoying it? Am I serving in the best way I can?" The feeling was always a green light.

I got a clear message: "Be yourself and make it fun! Don't take it so seriously!" This was the exact opposite of what our sponsor had instructed. He had stressed the importance of structure and how the Danish are sticklers for protocol. I confess the idea of "making it fun" really got my creative juices going, and I was immediately fueled with energy. It felt right. I remembered that using props and humorous role plays got other classes engaged and energized, so I decided to let out my Texas playful side.

My particular piece was on establishing credibility and negotiation as leaders — all pretty serious stuff. (That's what they thought.) I designed a contest using old-fashioned hotel service bells, dice, tequila lollipops, and rubber chickens. I actually tossed the squeaky, noise-making rubber chickens out to the groups when introducing the rules. (These caught my eye as I passed a pet store in Vienna while walking and feeling grateful for my life.) I don't know how I got the tequila lollipops, each with a worm, past airport security. Again, this is a sample of unlimited ideas. The participants absolutely loved the entire module. They were 100% present. They were creative and brave with their business tactics during the role plays. Most importantly, they learned and remembered sophisticated negotiation techniques. I was honored with the best scores of the week.

Again, the lesson here is: don't worry about what everyone else is doing, and just follow your unique brand of guidance. This gives you energy, power, and so much joy. An interesting side note: a few months later, one of the trainers called to tell me that he had tried to use rubber chickens in one of his training groups. He explained that it was a disaster and they made fun of him!

Another lesson to remember: Your guidance is very uniquely designed for you. It will enhance and showcase your one-of-a-kind combination of experiences. I happen to love toys. I'm 5 feet tall and a girl from Texas, so I wasn't embarrassed to use bells, chickens, and other props. Fun is one of my top 3 mandates in life. This style is part of my brand. Listen to your inner guidance above everyone else's. In my Mindset Mastery programs, we become experts at tuning out the external noise and creating shortcuts to your specific brand of success and happiness.

How Do You Know When It's The Real Thing?

How do you know when you are streaming true source guidance versus making decisions based on ego or fear? You will know by how you feel. It's like having a built-in compass in your heart, just like the magnetic needle of a compass aligns with the earth's magnetic field, causing it to point true north. Your feelings will also be crystal clear and align with what feels right. What feels in "alignment" with your true self? I say, "More alignment, less action gets you there faster." Getting into alignment first is paramount to moving forward with greater ease, happiness, and contentment. For example, before an important meeting or before sitting down to write an important piece, I take some quiet time, meditate and get aligned or in tune so I can stream my source. I plug into where all my answers exist.

True guidance usually has three qualities you can feel: Clarity, Calmness, and Joy.

The direction will be so crystal clear that it will give you a sense of contentment, energy, and peace of mind. Also, when you truly follow your intuition, you will do it happily and not really give too much attention to other people's opinions. (This is crucial because other people will say things based on their own personal fears and filters. Their map of the world is different from yours.)

You know it's the real thing because you will step into such a bold, resolved state of being that all normalcy and logic will go out the window, and no one can stop it—not even you. You'll be acting from a place of clarity and strength that vibrates on such a high energetic frequency that it creates any pathways and situations needed to reach its end destiny—an end result that is for the good of all.

How To Develop Your Connection To Source

1. **Create Quietness.** Make sure to carve out time consistently to hear your messages and intuition among all the noise out there. This is the step that most people don't take.

2. **Be in Surrender.** Do your best to be in a "green light" thinking mindset. This means not judging any ideas that may surface. Just go with the flow of consciousness, and you will be amazed.

3. **Practice Humility.** The moment you understand that you don't really do anything by yourself and that you are connected to the world and to all others, you can experience a huge release of responsibility and just be open to what comes to you.

4. **Tune Into Your Natural Curiosity.** There is huge power in curiosity. It means we are open and willing to go beyond our comfort zone, where our strength lies.

5. **Take Steps That Show You Listened.** This step is very important because it shows a sense of gratitude and trust in your inner voice. It also demonstrates there is a deep understanding of collaboration. Remember, movement creates movement. Ideas love movement. They don't like to just stay dormant. Ideas want to be heard, appreciated and shared!

"Ideas love movement."

Sandra Saenz

Your Divine Safety Net

Can you imagine living your life without ever having any doubt about your next step? That's what happens when you stream your source. Moving forward, knowing that you are never alone and being supported with a divine safety net in everything you do. At the core of my teachings is always the concept of connecting with your source power. Your finances, relationships, career, and health can exist as you wish and at your command. You harness a knowingness that is unlimited. Your Divine Source Stream is BETTER than Google. Google provides answers based on what has been in the past and data from third parties. But your Divine Source offers answers that are being created AS YOU WISH for them. Solutions and ideas that come into existence for the first time are activated by the power of your desire. You are powerful. THAT is your birthright.

To connect with Sandra:

For more information on Sandra's programs:

EMAIL: sandrasdreamteam@gmail.com

WEBSITE: www.dreamteamcommunications.com

LinkedIn: https://www.linkedin.com/in/saenzsandra

Facebook: https://www.facebook.com/sandra.saenz.169

Lifestyle Recode Program ®

Release & Reset 30 Day Series®

Mindset Mastery for Business Professionals®

Streaming Source Audio

Melissa S. O'Connell

Melissa is a *creative girl - turned corporate girl - turned life coach*. She grew up as a sensitive child who loved to draw and dance and dreamed of becoming an actress. Eventually she made her way to New York City, only to land in advertising, where a career in the corporate world spanning two decades then followed.

Along the way she remained the empathic and creative girl she'd always been at heart, but she struggled to be her true self in a world that seemed to ask her to forget her creativity and to keep her feelings to herself. After the birth of her daughter, she knew she had to become the "someone" she'd been looking for; a Creative Empath who would help empower other Empaths to embrace their gifts and make positive changes in their lives and work.

Melissa then became a certified Life Coach and founded her life coaching business "Creative Girl Helping the World", focusing on supporting Creative and Business Empaths.

Melissa pulls from her corporate experience, coaching skills and empathic abilities to help her clients navigate their life and work; guiding them to embrace and share their unique gifts, build authentic lives they love and to stay positive, productive and profitable in the process.

Melissa currently lives with her husband and daughter in the New York/New Jersey area.

The Biggest Obstacle We'll Ever Overcome

By Melissa S. O'Connell

"Maybe the journey isn't so much about becoming anything. Maybe it's about un-becoming everything that isn't really you, so you can be who you were meant to be in the first place."

-Paulo Coelho

Becoming Someone Else

I was recently interviewed about my work as a life coach where I was asked to share the biggest obstacle I had overcome in my life, that had made me who I am today.

Questions like these always take me back to my childhood. Looking back now, I know that's when I started un-becoming who I really was, to become, well, someone else.

I was born a highly sensitive, creative person; my childhood interests and dreams reflected that. I intuitively loved anything creative: drawing, painting, dancing, and acting, and I could get lost for hours using my imagination to pretend and create. I remember watching the musical "Singing in the Rain" with my grandmother when I was just five years old. It left me in complete amazement, and from then on, I had big plans to continue down my creative path and become an actress one day. But as so many of these stories go, I was discouraged by those around me from pursuing my creativity as a career or much further, as I got older. I want to believe that, deep down, their intentions were good and meant as a way to protect me because I was such a sensitive child, but as a result of this lack of support, I began to doubt myself and my abilities.

It marked the first time I'd ever felt that I couldn't be my true self or live my own life in the way I'd dreamed of doing.

From that time on, I realized that I began to shrink back from who I was and found ways to hide my sensitivity and my need to be creative. I couldn't help continuing with some of my creative outlets. Creating was truly an innate need, but I accepted that these should only be pursued as hobbies in my life so I could focus on getting a more realistic job. As time went on, I also found myself becoming afraid of pursuing the creative things that I once really loved, which served to create even more distance between who I really was and who I was now becoming. I also worked harder to hide my reactions when someone hurt my feelings or my shock when I saw how horribly some people treated others, because being so sensitive had always been this unfortunate flaw that I was told I had. I eventually went on to college to major in communications, taking art, acting, and dance classes on the side, of course, and then moved to New York City, where I landed a job at a top advertising agency.

It kicked off what I thought was a practical and safe (almost creative, but not too creative) career and a new life where I could move forward from my childhood into new possibilities.

Growing up, I'd never heard the term "empath." So it wasn't until years later, in a desperate and depressed state of mind in my career and life, that I began to seek answers as to why I was the way I was and why I was so unhappy. Discovering that I was an "empath" finally gave me an identity that I could align with, instead of feeling like an overly sensitive outsider who still felt destined for something more meaningful, rather than an office job working long hours for what seemed to be a shallow purpose.

Suddenly, all of my individual strengths, my big emotions and deep empathy for others, the ability to feel the energy all around me, my sense of intuition, the way I creatively solved problems, and how I viewed the world made more sense to me. But so did my challenges, my inability to set firm boundaries, my tendency to people please and over-apologize so others would like me, my constant struggle with never having enough energy, and the need for a lot of alone time.

I finally started to understand who I was and to connect with myself again.

Un-becoming Who We've Become

The biggest obstacle I've ever faced is finding my way back to being my true, creative, and feeling self, to being me again.

For many years, I dreamed of living in New York City to work in advertising agencies and the corporate and fashion worlds. I succeeded in doing that for nearly 20 years, and because of that, I know what it's like to be a Creative Empath trying to find balance, personal fulfillment, and success in work and life. On the outside, it all looked great, but being truly honest, it wasn't easy, and I still struggled constantly.

I did the best I could, existing and operating in my life and work the only way I knew how, but now with a stronger sense of who I was and why. I went on to spend nearly two decades in the corporate world, working for several companies in the areas of digital, e-commerce, fashion, technology, and operations. During that time, I learned to use my empathic and creative abilities as strengths that helped me succeed in my jobs and set me apart as someone with something unique to offer in her work. Along the way, I also met many people like me, those who were creative and had big feelings, who sensed there was more for them, and who had my energy challenges. It was the first time I learned just how important it is, especially as an empath, to find a tribe of like-minded and feeling people that I could relate to and who understood me.

Connecting with and supporting those in my tribe was the most significant positive factor that helped me through all of the years I spent in the corporate world.

Many times throughout my childhood and into my career, I'd been told that I shouldn't be so sensitive, that I'm being too passionate, or that I should learn not to take things so personally. The people providing this feedback were probably well-intentioned and trying to help me find ways to better cope with the situations I encountered in my work and life. But this kind of advice only frustrated me further. It also made me realize that this seemed to be the way that almost everyone was telling themselves and those around them to handle their feelings, serving as a message to deny who we truly are in order to be able to function in our lives and work.

I saw another side where people wanted to feel their feelings and not be separated from their creativity and authentic selves. I remember thinking one day when I'd returned to my job after maternity leave for my now 8-year-old daughter, that "someone" should do something about this…and then I reminded myself that I am someone! Spending a few months away from work with my new daughter helped me reflect on where I was now in my life. My intuition was loudly telling me that I needed to serve everyone around me in a more significant and even more authentic way. Later that same year while I was still in my corporate career, I decided to become a certified life coach. It took me almost another year of studying at night after work and on the weekends to complete my certification, but it's an accomplishment that I'm incredibly proud of.

I was drawn to becoming a life coach because I now understood that it was part of my responsibility to bring awareness and resolution to some of the issues I'd encountered as a creative empath in my work and life, in a bigger and more impactful way. Creativity and compassion are human superpowers that will help us save ourselves and the world if we embrace them and become what they can empower us to be. I also believe we should take things personally, because we're all living this life together. The energy and attitudes we show up with impact everyone around us daily, whether we realize it or not. And I remembered all of those who had been a part of my empath tribe throughout my career, who, like me, were seeking understanding, support, and a place to just be their true selves.

I wanted to become the "someone" who helped other empaths feel empowered to make positive and needed changes in their work and life circumstances.

Becoming Who We Are Meant To Be

Mine has not been a typical career path for a highly creative and empathetic person. But I believe that each experience in life can teach you something and that you can contribute your unique gifts to any situation. I've realized that everything I've learned and experienced up to this point in my life was to prepare me for my next calling as a life coach. After becoming certified, I founded my life coaching business, "Creative Girl Helping the World," and I'm a life coach for empaths, focusing on supporting creative and business empaths.

This work that I'm truly passionate about, is near and dear to my heart because I know first-hand the struggles that my empath clients face. Helping them to lead happier, more authentic lives is work that I'm proud of and called to be on. As a creative empath myself, I pull from my corporate experience, coaching skills, creativity, and empathic abilities to help my empath clients navigate their lives and work, empowering them to thrive along the way.

My mission is to help creative empaths embrace their unique gifts as their superpowers and use them to create an authentic life they love, fully in alignment with the creativity and empathy they were born to share with the world.

We have so many amazing gifts to share - we shouldn't have to settle for being drained of our energy or dulling our empathic abilities just to get through our work and lives every day. Being a creative empath, I've learned and believe it doesn't have to be this way. I know the artistic perspective, the intuitive nature and the deep feelings we bring into everything we do in our lives - and I can't imagine being any other way! But I also know about the challenges, frustrations, doubts and criticism we face daily while trying to navigate our lives as a highly creative and sensitive person. It's my goal to help creative empaths understand that our world needs us to share all of our gifts, so we can all learn and heal from the examples of self-expression, vision, intuition, empathy, and so much more that we show those around us every day when we're empowered to live as our authentic selves.

There's also another side to my mission. While I'm helping to empower creative empaths to be their authentic selves, I also feel it's important that those who are our friends, family, and work colleagues also understand who we are, what we need, and what we have to offer. To accomplish this, we must fully own and embrace being creative empaths in our lives and work. Sharing who we truly are with our loved ones, friends, and work colleagues is one of the first steps in doing this, and it also helps to educate them on how to best support us so we can, in turn, be our best for them.

To help continue this conversation, I'm including some of the key ways that we as creative empaths can empower ourselves, as well as a few important points for our loved ones and work colleagues to know and remember about our unique gifts and how we can contribute.

Here are some of the many ways that you can empower yourself as a creative empath:

- Your energy is your greatest asset in life and work, so learn to manage it and to make self-care a priority.
- Find a tribe of like-minded, supportive, creative empaths whom you can connect with on a deeper level.
- Practice setting boundaries to help protect your energy, prevent people-pleasing and to help you say "no" when you need to.
- Celebrate your accomplishments, practice sharing them with others, as well as your feelings and your creativity.
- Yes, you are different, but in the best ways, so use your unique gifts as superpowers in your life and work.

And for those who want to support a creative empath in your life or at work, here are some important points to know and remember.

In life:

- Let them feel and express their many feelings; don't downplay, belittle, or deny them.

- Be understanding when they need quiet, alone time to recharge their energy.
- Remember that they're constantly feeling energy, which can overwhelm them when in big crowds, during sad movies, seeing negative news, after a long, busy day, etc.
- Support their dreams, creative outlets and business endeavors, no matter how big or small they may seem; your support is invaluable to them.
- Understand that their empathic feelings, creativity, sensing of energy, etc. are innate abilities for them and aren't characteristics that they can simply "turn off."

In work:

- These are some of your best team members and assets because of their naturally high level and range of Emotional Intelligence (EQ)
- Make them leaders so they can use their empathy to nurture team members, cross-functional collaboration and business relationships.
- Allow them to problem-solve in their own unique way, using their creativity and intuition to uncover hidden issues or imagine solutions for business challenges.
- They are great listeners and observers, allowing them to easily understand client pain points or the details needed to complete a project.
- Remember that they're energy-driven, which means their work timing and output levels may differ by the day, so give them flexibility in their schedule and time to recharge.

While growing up and building my career, I didn't always understand what I now know with absolute certainty: that we are the true and best source for understanding who we are and what we need in our lives. We go through so much in life that chips away at who we really are, causing us to slowly become something else; shaped by the opinions of others, the way we make a living, the relationships we have, and the ways we have to adapt to survive in life.

But we are creative empaths! Anyone with the gifts of creativity and empathy (and so much more!) should never be afraid to use them. This means becoming fully empowered to be our true authentic selves, to share the talents and gifts we have with others, to find our calling and purpose in life, and to achieve our dreams!

***

To contact Melissa:

-Website: https://www.creativegirlhelpingtheworld.com

-Email: melissa@creativegirlhelpingtheworld.com

-Facebook: https://www.facebook.com/MelSOConnell

-Instagram: https://www.instagram.com/melsoconnell

-LinkedIn: https://www.linkedin.com/in/melissasoconnell

Annie Mood

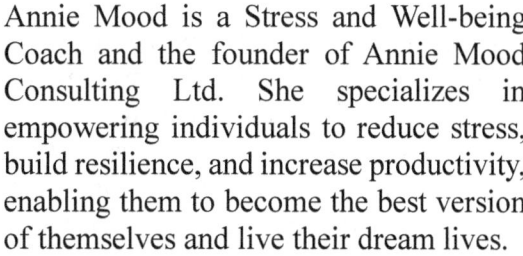

Annie Mood is a Stress and Well-being Coach and the founder of Annie Mood Consulting Ltd. She specializes in empowering individuals to reduce stress, build resilience, and increase productivity, enabling them to become the best version of themselves and live their dream lives.

With over 22 years of experience in education, Annie has enjoyed a career in the classroom and served as a Special Education Needs Advisor for Autism and Social, Emotional Mental Health. Her expertise also extends to being a Reiki Master, HeartMath Coach, and Emotional Freedom Technique Practitioner. In addition, Annie has a Bachelor of Science (BSc) in Business Management and IT.

Annie's dedication to personal development impelled her collaboration with a colleague on the 'nattylala' technique. This innovative approach aimed to empower children to effectively manage their emotions and attain their optimal learning state, fostering academic success. She then co-authored the book "A New Approach for Calm Classrooms: Do the Nattylala with Silent Tapping" and successfully implemented this technique with students in various schools.

In addition to her professional achievements, Annie has overcome her own challenges, including conquering her fear of public speaking and raising a child with a rare profile of autism known as Pathological Demand Avoidance. Despite the challenges of single motherhood, she persevered on her healing journey, mastering the art of self-love.

From Adversity to Empowerment – Own Your Power
by Annie Mood

Boom! Boom! Boom! On the door. "They're coming. They're coming to take our homes!" I was merely four years old, growing up in apartheid South Africa, when my neighbor pounded on our door, exclaiming that a riot was erupting, and the 'Black' South Africans were advancing to reclaim our homes. It was the moment when overwhelming sadness and fear engulfed me. The room dimmed in my young eyes, and all I could sense was trembling terror. My mother feared she would lose me that night, as I couldn't cease shaking, and she felt powerless to soothe me and provide a sense of safety. That pivotal moment in my life entrenched a profound sense of FEAR within me—an apprehension for life and a dread of people. It became the formidable dragon I had to combat to navigate the world as myself.

As a timid schoolgirl, fear led me to transform into a selective mute. I found myself incapable of speaking to others; I could barely manage a whisper in my teacher's ear. I became one of those inconspicuous children in the classroom, avoiding praise, shunning the spotlight, and preferring invisibility. I was repeatedly dismissed as excessively shy and unmistakably deemed lacking in intelligence by numerous authority figures, fueling my profound sense of poor self-worth.

Growing up in a country that reinforced my Indian heritage of inferiority and low self-worth, change was a foreign concept. Taught that having lighter skin meant being superior to those with darker tones and that deeper skin tones indicated a greater sense of inferiority; the cultural expectation was to accept one's fate.

However, nestled deep within me, there was a flicker of spark—an ember of longing to become someone, something, not merely a nothing. So here I was, emerging from school as a modest C-average student; the notion of my acceptance into a teacher training college shocked many acquainted with me. "Seriously? You!" I can still envision the disbelief etched on numerous faces to this day.

However, deep within me, hidden from my conscious awareness, a flicker of potential remained dormant, defying the expectations imposed by society. It surfaced for the first time upon completing my teaching qualifications—a surprising spark that kindled an unexpected resolve within me. It impelled me to embark on a journey to England. I had never set foot on an airplane, never ventured beyond the safety of my parents' embrace, and never dared to explore the world alone. Yet, the spark held sway, and within three months of deciding to depart from South Africa, I found myself bound for England, propelled by a newfound courage to embrace change.

A New Beginning

Embarking on a new chapter in a foreign country, far from the confines of my segregated culture in South Africa, stirred within me a tumult of emotions. The mere thought of conversing openly with someone of a different race sparked bewilderment. Could I genuinely engage with a 'white' person without reservation? What words would I utter, and how would I be perceived? The ghost of selective mutism returned, gripping me in its silent embrace. Only when spoken to would I muster the courage to respond. Yet, amidst the uncertainty, the spark within me reignited, illuminating my path forward.

The mystery of self-worth resided in its elusive nature. Despite accolades and career achievements, I found myself wrestling with a feeling of insufficiency. This affliction can affect many of us, stemming from how we perceive ourselves in the intricate fabric of society.

Unbeknownst to us, this internal narrative of unworthiness often dictates our decisions. From career choices to our demeanor in the world, from the relationships we cultivate to the depth of joy we allow ourselves to experience, and even to the abundance we permit ourselves to receive—each decision bears the imprint of our self-perception.

I came to the profound realization that self-worth is a construct—a program crafted from life's experiences, something we absorb and internalize over time. And if it is something we can learn, then it follows that we can also unlearn it.

Thus commenced a journey of unlearning and reprogramming—an odyssey to reshape my perceptions of race, people, culture, and, most importantly, self-esteem and self-worth. Self-worth, the base of personal validation, emerged as the cornerstone of my quest for success.

Now, I want to offer you the culmination of many years spent learning, discovering myself, healing, and empowering myself—a condensed method that could support your self-empowerment journey. However, before we proceed, it's crucial to grasp the concepts of self-worth, self-confidence, and self-esteem for clarity.

Self-worth is a fundamental aspect of our lives, yet its significance often goes unnoticed. This internal belief system acts as our personal law of attraction, shaping the experiences and opportunities we manifest. It encapsulates our innate sense of value and deservingness. Initially high in infants, it gradually evolves as they absorb external influences such as societal norms and cultural expectations.

Conversely, self-confidence pertains to our faith in our skills and capabilities, cultivated through knowledge, experience, and self-awareness. For instance, individuals seasoned in their profession convey confidence in their abilities.

Meanwhile, self-esteem reflects the evaluation we make of ourselves, encompassing our perceived importance and significance. Despite possessing remarkable talents, many individuals fail to connect them with personal value, resulting in the undervaluation of their products and services in business and careers—a phenomenon intricately linked with self-worth.

Embarking on a journey to self-worth necessitated a profound exploration of the subconscious. It entailed delving into the intricate layers of programming and initiating a transformative decluttering process. In this context, decluttering signifies discarding what no longer serves one's growth and retaining only what empowers and uplifts.

The Decluttering to Empowering Process

Let's break it down to its simplest form.

Continuous Growth - Think of personal growth as a never-ending journey. We evolve to a higher level each time we let go of old beliefs or habits. And there's always more to learn and shed as we keep growing.

Discovering Purpose - Our purpose is to become the best version of ourselves. It's a choice we make, even though it might feel uncomfortable at times. Remember, we're all a work in progress, and that's completely normal.

Understanding Polarity - Our world operates on the idea of opposites. We'll feel the tug of these opposing forces within ourselves and in the world around us.

Changing Beliefs - Reprogramming our subconscious starts with self-reflection. Instead of focusing on why we think a certain way, it's more important to understand what beliefs hold us back and how to change them.

Taking Ownership - Rather than blaming our past or circumstances, we can take responsibility for our happiness. We now have the tools to break free from old patterns and create a more fulfilling life.

Letting Go of the Past - The person we used to be is just that— the past. We can choose to leave behind old habits and beliefs whenever we're ready. It's about embracing change and embracing the opportunity for growth.

The Art of Self-Exploration – Uncovering Our Unconscious Choices

The next part consists of a 2-step process to assist in identifying the unconscious choices you may be making. When undertaking this exercise, it's crucial to be honest with yourself. Being honest with yourself is vital because self-awareness and self-honesty are essential for personal growth and development. Without honesty, you may overlook important aspects of your behaviour or mindset that need attention, hindering your ability to make meaningful changes. Being honest with yourself allows you to identify areas for improvement, confront uncomfortable truths, and ultimately make more informed decisions that align with your values, purpose, and goals.

Step 1 - Notice

Examining Results –

Evaluate the results you are experiencing in your life. They serve as the primary indicator of whether your current programming is beneficial or unfavourable. Suppose you find yourself leading an abundant, joyful, and purposeful life, feeling worthy. In that case, it suggests that you have either transformed your negative programming or possess a mindset rooted in high self-worth. Your results offer insights into your internal dynamics.

Actions and Habits -

Assess your daily activities. Are you navigating life without considering the repercussions of your actions on others, yourself, and your physical health? For example, adults have expressed a lack of education regarding healthy eating habits. Thus, a pertinent question arises: What impedes you, as a self-reliant adult, from shifting from unhealthy dietary patterns to more wholesome ones? Therefore, it is imperative to prioritize the examination of your habits and actions.

Mindset –

The mind functions as a skilled storyteller, crafting narratives that shape our perceptions and beliefs. It's crucial to cultivate mindfulness regarding the thoughts we entertain and the stories we construct internally. Are these narratives akin to "I've never been taught to eat healthy," or "You're going to die anyway, so why bother eating well?" or "I don't have time to cook because I work 16 hours a day"? Remember, you are not synonymous with your mind. You possess a mind, but you are distinct from it. Thus, it's imperative not to unquestioningly accept every narrative it presents.

Emotions –

Your emotions serve as significant indicators of the messages your mind is conveying. It may be inundating you with fear, highlighting all the potential pitfalls, or presenting a myriad of possibilities for success. Often, it's a blend of both. When negative thoughts stemming from subconscious programming dominate your mind, negative emotions follow suit. Hence, when experiencing negative emotions, consider journaling to unravel the narratives your mind is feeding you.

Step 2 – Investigate

As you begin to observe the impact of your programming in your daily life, you can shift the dynamic by fostering curiosity through investigation. What precisely are you exploring? Identify beliefs that hinder your progress and those that empower you. This step is paramount, as it unveils hidden barriers and potential sources of strength. You can't address what you're unaware of until you become aware. Once you do, the power lies in choosing, adapting, and acting.

Why get curious? - Curiosity serves to eliminate judgment. As human beings, we often criticize ourselves for not meeting certain standards. However, during this phase, it's crucial to approach ourselves with honesty, truthfulness, and compassion, just as we would treat a cherished loved one. Embracing curiosity allows us to explore without preconceived notions, enabling insights to naturally surface as we engage with questions and observations.

To achieve this, pose these questions to yourself. Journaling proves to be the most effective method, allowing a pause between your thoughts and their transcription. This delay provides valuable time for processing information and gaining deeper insights.

1. How do I currently feel?

2. What activates these emotions? Are they linked to a genuine problem or merely speculative concerns?

3. What thoughts occupy my mind at present? Given the vast number of thoughts we think daily, it's likely to be a mixture of positive and negative thoughts. Remember, our thoughts greatly influence our emotional state.

4. How do I behave? For instance, do I lash out in anger, fear, worry, or stress? Compile a list of daily actions to pinpoint any recurring habits, attitudes, or behaviors. Evaluate whether they contribute positively to your growth, such as exercise and meditation, or hinder it, like excessive sugar intake or irregular sleep patterns.

5. What life stage am I currently navigating? This factor significantly shapes our thoughts, emotions, and daily routines. For instance, parenthood may prioritize family well-being and financial stability, while menopause could influence hormonal fluctuations and related concerns.

6. Am I aligned with my life's purpose? In what way am I living my purpose?

7. How do I define success, and am I currently achieving it?

8. Do I establish goals and follow through with their execution? How can I ascertain my progress in this regard?

Step 3 - Action

Once you've observed and cultivated curiosity about your thoughts, emotions, habits, and results, it's time to initiate action. At this stage, you're acting from a place of knowledge.

One effective approach I recommend is tapping into the subconscious to release limiting beliefs and reprogram with empowering ones. While there are numerous methods available, I'll walk you through one that has yielded remarkable results for me, my clients, and even children experiencing trauma, as well as in educational settings. It's called Emotional Freedom Technique (EFT).

Summary of Emotional Freedom Technique (EFT)

EFT is a method of Restoring Energy Flow for Emotional Well-being

Unresolved negative emotions stored in the body create energy disturbances, leading to feelings of discomfort, stress, and illness. Through tapping on specific meridian points, EFT restores the natural flow of energy, promoting clarity of thought, confident decision-making, stress reduction, and alignment with our highest good. Tapping can be performed with or without verbal cues, making it accessible for various individuals, including children and individuals who struggle to find the right words.

Moreover, EFT offers a powerful method for reprogramming old negative beliefs and instilling empowering new ones. Individuals can release emotional blockages and disrupt ingrained patterns by tapping on specific meridian points while focusing on negative beliefs. This process allows for integrating positive affirmations and beliefs, fostering a shift towards greater self-worth, resilience, and alignment with personal growth goals.

I'll provide a brief overview of the tapping points. Please refer to the diagram below for a visual representation of these points.

The 9 EFT Tapping Points

Tapping without verbal cues. Tap gently about 5-7 times.

1. Karate Chop Point – on the blade of the hand between the little finger and wrist
2. Corner of Eyebrow – the point where the eyebrow meets the top of the nose
3. Side of the eye – on the bone bordering the outer corner of the eye, in line with the pupil
4. Under the eye – on the bone under the eye, in line with the pupil
5. Under the nose – in the little hollow that is called the philtrum
6. Under the lip – between the bottom lip and chin
7. Collarbone – where the breastbone and collarbone meet
8. Under the arm – on the side of the body, directly under the armpit
9. Top of the head – in the middle of the crown

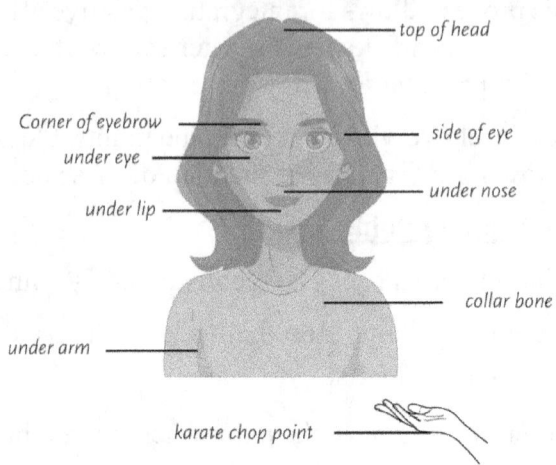

Tapping with Verbal Cues

Here's a simplified process for doing Emotional Freedom Technique (EFT) tapping:

1. Identify the issue - Think about a specific problem or emotion you want to address. It could be anxiety, stress, fear, or any other negative feeling.

2. Rate the intensity - On a scale of 0 to 10, rate the intensity of the emotion or issue you're experiencing. This helps you track your progress throughout the tapping process.

3. Setup statement - Create a setup statement acknowledging the problem while accepting yourself. For example: "Even though I feel anxious about this situation, I deeply and completely love and accept myself."

4. Tap on the karate chop point - Using two fingers, tap the karate chop point on the side of your hand while repeating your setup statement three times.

5. Tapping sequence - Tap on the specific meridian points on your body while stating your issue or affirmations. The sequence includes the corner of the eyebrow, the side of the eye, under the eye, under the nose, under the lip, the collarbone, under the arm, and the top of the head. (see the illustration above). Repeat the sequence three to seven times.

6. Reassess the intensity - After completing the tapping sequence, reassess the intensity of your issue on a scale of 0 to 10. This helps measure the energy flow through your body.

7. Repeat if necessary - If the intensity hasn't decreased to your desired level, repeat the tapping sequence while adjusting your setup statement or affirmations as needed.

8. Final assessment - Once you feel a significant reduction in intensity or complete relief, reassess the intensity of your issue one final time to ensure you've effectively addressed it.

Remember, EFT tapping may require practice and experimentation to find what works best for you. Feel free to adapt the process to suit your individual needs and preferences.

Conclusion

As I have navigated through life, I've encountered the formidable force of fear. It's often felt like an insurmountable obstacle, capable of either breaking me or defining me. However, I've discovered a profound truth. Fear can be a catalyst for transformation. By facing it head-on, engaging in meaningful dialogue, and delving into its depths, I've learned to harness its energy to drive me forward. With courage as my trusted ally, I embarked on a journey towards self-worth, knowing that every step taken in the face of fear is a step towards growth and empowerment. As I navigate this path, I hope to inspire others to embrace their fears and discover the boundless possibilities that emerge when fear is embraced as a friend.

As you reflect on your journey, consider how embracing fear as a catalyst for transformation empowers you to unlock your full potential and live a life of purpose and fulfillment so that you can Own Your Power.

To contact Annie:

Annie Mood Consulting ltd

https://linktr.ee/anniemood

website: anniemood.newzenler.com

Instagram - https://www.instagram.com/anniemoodconsulting/

LinkedIn - https://www.linkedin.com/in/annie-mood-coaching/

Facebook Group - https://www.facebook.com/groups/anniemoodcoaching

email – info@anniemood.com

phone - +447774313451

Lynne Hurlburt

Lynne Hurlburt was an entrepreneur in the Denver, Colorado, metro area for over 26 years. She taught business seminars, business coached, and owned over six brick-and-mortar businesses for more than 25 years in the beauty, restaurant, and service industries.

Her positive energy was addicting in Colorado. As a savvy business owner, philanthropist, and politician, she helped grow three suburban towns in south Denver. She was one of Denver's most well-known socialites.

She was featured in a non-fiction book called "Lessons from the Business Heroes of the Pandemic" written by Duane McHodgkins in 2020.

She retired in 2022 and moved to south Texas by the beach to be with family. She continues to dabble in business... and is working on 2 fiction books.

You can follow her interesting life on any social media platform as "Lynne Hurlburt."

Don't Stop

By Lynne Hurlburt

Chapter one

Have you ever thought about how you would end it? I mean, leave all you have done and accomplished and quickly walk away. Retired. Just like that.

As entrepreneurs, there is no end. We are not wired to just stop. I remember when a business trend was to "have an exit plan." I never even had the right answer. Other entrepreneurs had an exit plan. I listened, and it seemed legitimate, but it still never helped me feel hopeful I would ever find my exit plan.

I felt my business life like I felt my family life. It was a part of me as much as God and family. The highs and lows, fears and failures, and most of all ...the wins.

I hope you find peace in reading my life journey of struggles that compelled me to adapt to change.

Chapter Two

I was born and raised in a small town in Iowa. I was the youngest of 3 with both parents. My parents did not have a lot of money, but we had what we needed. We had no heat upstairs – so we did not spend time in our bedrooms. Scorching summers and bitterly cold winters.

Two weeks before my senior year in high school, my father died in the middle of the night from a heart attack. I awoke before he fell off the bed. Then I heard my mom coming upstairs to get my brother- who was in college home for the summer. I could not save him and stayed calm for my mother until the first responders got there. I was daddy's girl. I knew I would stay strong for my mother. My senior high school years were a blur. I saw myself growing stronger. We had community, church, and family. I was the one responsible for taking care of my mother. I saw her getting stronger each week. Growing up was not an option.

I left for college. My mom would be okay. She had my sister and brother-in-law to take care of her. They were her rock until she passed 25 years later.

Chapter Three

I moved to Colorado when I was 23 with my "on and off "high school boyfriend. I did not know this would be the best decision of my life. There are so many opportunities in a big city. I broke up with my boyfriend after six months of living with him. I did not want to be his wife.

I worked in a fast-paced franchise salon in Boulder Colorado. I worked my way up fast and made it the #1 salon out of 2,800 salons in the franchise. Corporate saw my numbers and offered me an excellent job to help franchisees and be a trainer. I opened 99 salons.

I dated and partied after working over 10-hour days six days a week. I was young and cocky. Fast success makes you that way. I thought I knew it all. Then, as a trainer in the Denver market and managing managers, I was humbled daily by making bad choices. I never disrespected anyone because I needed them and was always fair. I learned how to get back up when I made a mistake. I learned how to fake it and became a great leader. Emotional intelligence was necessary.

Chapter Four

I fell in love with a nice guy and had two daughters. After being a mom, I could not get back into the grind of business life after speaking with daycare centers. I opened my first business while working part-time with the franchise chain for which I had lived. I worked around my husband's weird work schedule. But I made it work. I worked more while the kids were at school. I was scared but excited. My husband made good money for me to be able to take the chance. I worked late nights after the kids and husband were in bed. He was always incredibly supportive.

As the years went by, I opened other businesses in other industries. My kids and husbands' schedules made me an organized "queen." I was happy thriving in my passions while being a mother, so I made no time for myself.

The Change

The kids went off to college, and I worked more. My husband drank more alcohol. He worked more, too, so we had money for their college. My marriage was crumbling. I did not know what to do, so I did nothing but build my business empire. Our daughters saw us growing apart when they visited home and mentioned we should get divorced. I told my husband, "We need marriage counseling, and you need to stop drinking." He was so addicted to alcohol that he would not agree. I poured my life into my employees and my businesses instead of our marriage.

Another change that I knew I could not miss a beat. Or I would lose everything I had worked so hard for the past 20-plus years. We divorced two years later, and I was prepared. My husband was not, so I helped him move to an apartment on his own. I picked his furniture out and took him shopping so he could learn to date. I had taken care of him in our marriage, so I knew he would struggle, and the change would be extremely hard on him. He quit caring about his career and spent most of his time drinking alone.

I did not mention this to my employees or people in my business world. I was desensitized to my pain. I spent time alone after work, running at the gym and working on myself. I had time to develop better habits. I learned how to organize and plan my life. I read many self-help books and was blessed with single girlfriends. I learned a lot from them about being alone. I asked many questions about their lifestyles.

These are the most critical changes that I made into habits:

Self-care and alone time to reflect, set up networking/social quality, eat healthy (8020 rule), exercise 5-7 days a week, read (business and self-help) no watching television, planned and prioritized every day, learned new skills, took coaching classes/seminars, tracked my finances, wrote down my goals, developed mourning/night routines, prioritized sleep, volunteered more, cooked at home and invested in my future= mentally, physically and financially.

I saw myself turning into the woman I loved. I restructured all my businesses, and it showed. I sat on many non-profit boards. My brand was ME. I volunteered in the three towns where my businesses were located. I am certain everyone around me saw me fly.

I organized my life to be successful. I took at least five classes a month on personal development, and I made what I learned my intentional routines.

Chapter five

In February 2020, I felt something unusual happening in the community, but I could not put my finger on it. However, I always talked to my clients while I was doing their hair. The big companies that employed my clients were preparing them to work at home. I became obsessed with it. I read every night about a pandemic that was happening around the world.

I went to my millionaire monthly mastermind meeting in Denver. We all talked about how something big and different was about to happen. Then I started discussing it with my customers and found out more information about it.

I sat on the Governor's workforce committee and attended the meeting in March. Everyone was speculating about a shutdown by the end of March because of some pandemic. I kept it quiet in the towns I did business in. I knew most of my friends, customers, and employees would think I was nuts. I could not even grasp what a shutdown would look like. So, I kept doing business as usual while I read about it nightly.

Then it happened. I had customers coming in, mentioning we would be closed by Wednesday. My businesses were unusually busy. I listened. I worked over 12 hours Monday and Tuesday.

After work, I researched everything I could get my hands on. On Tuesday, one businessperson customer messaged me on Facebook: "Be ready for tomorrow." I respected him.

The next day, I headed to work, which was super busy for a Wednesday. I was not on the schedule but told my employees I would be back after my chamber leads networking meeting. I knew they would let customers know.

At the chamber meeting, everyone asked, "Our person presenting is not able to make it today, so what should we do, Lynne?" I always had answers because I pulled interesting stuff about business trends to pass around. So, they all looked at me for answers. I replied, "Let's go around and talk about what we will do with our business when we get shut down because of the pandemic."

They all looked at me in disbelief. But they knew I did my homework and knew a lot of businesspeople around Denver. A couple of business owners laughed at me and said, "They will not shut America down. No way would that ever happen." I responded, "Okay, hypothetically, let's discuss what we would do if it happened." No one was prepared and too scared to respond. But I made them talk about the uncertainty. I really had no fear and found the business world quite interesting. I threw out tons of questions to make them think about it so they would be prepared.

I headed back to my salon, and it was crazy busy. I called my daughter in college 8 hours away and told her that she might think of driving home. The salon was in panic mode. I kept my cool, so my employees followed. We all worked until 10 pm. I sent my exhausted employees home, and I cleaned. After, I sat down to read my emails before driving home. I read the one from the state regulatory agency telling me I had no business license, nor did I have any other professional license, and to shut down or stand getting all my licenses revoked permanently.

I text my employees, telling them not to come to work tomorrow and to read their emails.

The next morning, I called my attorney with questions. I sent a text memo out on instructions so they would not have any financial disruptions. They always worked so hard for me. I wanted them taken care of. I promised them it would be okay.

I knew why I had always saved my profits. It was because of something like this.

I remodeled a couple of my businesses during the shutdown. I had the time. Luckily, I signed up for DoorDash on a weekend the prior year as I was researching their app to start a beauty industry employment app. So, I was able to DoorDash eight plus hours a day in between my remodels. I did not know how long the shutdown would last, and I wanted to save as much money as possible.

I thought of a way to capture people stuck at home. So, I put my business coupons in the food bags as I delivered them. By researching other countries and how they were adapting, I decided to prepare for the opening. I stalked up on supplies after seeing other countries' protocols for businesses. I knew shortages would happen. Little did I know that prices would jump, so I saved a ton of money by being ahead of the game. I almost thought of everything. I went above state guidelines to keep my customers and employees safe. I spent my days door-dashing, remodeling, and texting/calling my customers.

I realized how important social media was. Covid made it more important. I posted pictures and updates on what I was doing. My employees kept updated that way, too.

I learned what zoom was and networked online. And other events. At first there were only a few community leaders online. But as I posted about it more chimed in.

I learned a lot about adapting. Fast. To survive. Something uncertain was exciting. I had business owners in my community wanting help and answers. It helped me to be helpful. I would meet them in the parking lot at one of my businesses.

Chapter Nine

I managed to drive down to Corpus Christi, Texas, a few times during the shutdown to visit my family. And get some beach, boat, and pool time. Texas was a lot more open than Colorado, so I felt peaceful and at home. I slowed down, and I really liked it.

Then, Colorado reopened, and I was back in the grind. It was interesting and different from all the uncertainties. I knew I would be okay. Each time I was in Texas, I had a weird feeling that I would not be in the grind much longer.

After months of trying to deal with the new normal, I had buyers who wanted my business. I thought about it all and caved in. I never had a plan to stop or retire. I loved most of everything I did.

I decided to walk away from it all. The uncertainty of everything made me realize, "do it, walk away." My employees, customers, great friends, and fans were all shocked. But I knew I would be okay, and so would they. It was them that made my success. They were my best critics, and they made me stronger and better. I loved trying new things and new ways to do business. They were always honest and did not always tell me what I wanted to hear. It was best that way. I made myself better and do better.

I sold my house and 80% of my belongings. It was just stuff. It was a refreshing feeling. I did not know how good it would feel until I did it.

Chapter 10

I have a new start. What a change! Entrepreneurs do not just stop doing what they love. I get to learn a new way of living. Freedom, more time. Less work, more hobbies.

I did not go into detail about the little changes in my life. But the little one's compound makes substantial changes easier. Write them down daily, weekly, and monthly on how to improve. I did not know that my father dying in my arms would shape my life and help me to be so strong when dealing with change.

Remember to always work on yourself. To be healthy for everyone and everything in your life.

I am working on being closer to God. I will get there. I always do. Funny how you put your blessings and God on the back burner. I am not forgetting, just not making him a priority, but I am here right now because God put me here to find him again. And I will. I am slowly learning how. My church is important to me. I am taking baby steps. Mostly because everyone seems to be a pro with God in my church, and I know I will be one day, too. Hanging around the pros will help me become one. I am going with the "you are who you hang with" attitude.

I golf, work out more, and do hair part-time in a fast-paced franchise salon. It helps me learn about my new community and network. I dabble in start-ups in business now, only smaller.

I started a women's professional non-profit group and a mastermind think tank so I can talk about business stuff. Business in the deep south is a new and different culture. I am fascinated by it.

I am a business coach for the city/government. It keeps my mind sharp, active, and involved in my new community. I volunteer and am still a Rotarian.

I live close to both of my daughters. I will keep my old friends while I am meeting new friends. I am lucky to live in a tourist town with my family. I don't have an end, yet. I have not finished.....

Catch me on any social media platform. My name is my brand.

Lynne Hurlburt

To contact Lynn:

Find me on

Facebook, Insta, TikTok, twitter @Lynne Hurlburt

Moon Sade

Moon Sade is an Autism Success Mentor who is passionate about guiding and empowering young adult autistics aged 17-25, alongside their families, through the complexities of their journey into adulthood. She integrates 25+ years of personal experience with certifications in Understanding Autism, Life Coaching, NLP, and Timeline Therapy, together with her years of experience as a high school teacher, gaining profound insight into her clients' specific challenges. She offers personalised mentoring suited to each individual's distinct aspirations and challenges. Dedicated to raising the profile of young adult autistics and their families, Moon has been a guest on various podcasts, including "On the Edge with April Mahoney" and recently on Women's Radio as the guest of neurodiversity campaigner Dr. Anna Kennedy OBE on her show "All Things Autism." She has been featured on the cover of Hoinser Media Group's "Top 50 Innovators 2023" issue, as well as been a featured speaker at Expert Channel TV's #ConsciousWealthSummit2023, as well as recently joined Expert Channel TV as an Expert Panelist, Expert Contributor, and a Member of the Board of Experts. Grounded in adaptability, compassion, and an unwavering commitment to fostering fundamental change, Moon empowers her clients to thrive independently.

Embracing Courage: My Journey of Awakening

By Moon Sade

"In the journey of a lifetime, one step forward every day is all it takes."

-Moon Sade

Looking back now, I can clearly see two faces—fear and courage—and how they shaped my choices in life, for worse and for better. One of those faces might be shaping your choices right now. The question is, which one?

I ask the question, but believe me, I understand it's not that easy to know the difference especially when your life and choices are being shaped by the face of fear wearing its sweetest, most reassuring mask.

Back then, in the years before my true story unfolded, before the turning point that put me on the path I walk today, I definitely didn't know the difference. I couldn't see how much fear was influencing my choices or my decisions for myself and my family.

I thought I was doing all the right things to build the best life for us.

In those years, I had an excellent job as a high school teacher. I enjoyed the teaching part of my job. Being in the classroom, experiencing those moments when 'my kids 'faces lit up with understanding and enjoyment - it was wonderful. The job paid well, and I was good at it. So good, that very early on, I was offered the opportunity to be trained to progress straight into senior management. I could hardly believe it! I'd only been in my role briefly, and opportunities like this didn't just come along. I'd be crazy to turn it away! In my heart of hearts, I knew that.

Yet, knowing that, instead of stepping forward and grasping the opportunity with both hands, I let fear dictate my choice and politely refused. Of course, I didn't see that fear was influencing my choice. At that point, I didn't know the two faces of the coin.

Instead, I told myself I couldn't take on the added responsibility because of my duty to my family; my young child needed me. After all, it would affect my working relationship with my colleagues who had been there longer than I had been, because it would upset the apple cart, and I didn't want to do that! I had so many seemingly perfectly plausible reasons I gave myself, but what I was really doing was playing it safe. I knew this opportunity would change my life in ways I couldn't foresee, but at that time, I didn't have the courage to step into the unknown. That came later when everything changed, and my true story began.

My story unfolds in two places at once, driven in different ways in both instances by my bright and uniquely individual autistic children. Eventually, circumstances built to a point where the "sweet little" reassuring face of the fear that had driven me for years finally unmasked itself and was revealed as the architect of the ever narrowing gap in the 'rock and the hard place 'that I had existed in for, what seemed like, forever.

Finally, in that moment, I clearly saw so many of my choices over the years for what they had been - choices driven by fear. Yes, in some instances, my fear had been influenced by a desire to keep us safe, but in other instances, my fear had sprung from the desire to keep hidden, not to be seen, to let others control my life, even if I didn't want them to because it was just easier that way.

At that moment, I had had enough of the same outcome, of the same repeating consequences of all those choices. I knew something had to change.

I watched my children—the eldest, already changed by years of dismissal and being misunderstood, and the younger, so innocent and sweet, but fated to walk the same path as his older brother, unless I grasped my courage, faced the unknown and stepped around the blind bend of the turning point in front of me and changed things.

Knowing the time was NOW, my heart was pounding like never before. I felt every quiver in my being as I looked into the raging face of the gaping fear in front of me. This time, though, instead of falling into my fear, I saw the other side of the coin - the courage to feel the fear and step forward anyway. I could feel that courage, propelling me, pushing me forward, filling me with determination, despite my uncertainty at the choice I knew I was about to make.

To understand my path now, you have to know the beginning, where it all started, more than 20 years ago, with my eldest child.

When my oldest was little, we noticed differences in how he did things: how he played with and without toys, interacted with people, reacted to things, and responded to what was happening around him. Small, slight differences, not so significant that they could be easily noticed or picked up on, but the type of signs parents notice, bringing with it the natural parental fear of what the future would hold for him and the desire to take steps to ensure these differences didn't stand in his way.

These early signs of developmental differences didn't fit the stereotypically expected ones of autism. He was a bright, intelligent child who, very early on, became a master at masking and mimicking. I raised our concerns with his educational providers, my voice small and quiet, deferential - despite my role as a full-time, experienced high school teacher. Our concerns were dismissed, ignored, and overlooked by those eager to see only what they wanted. And I? I was too afraid of the repercussions on my child, too worried about upsetting the apple cart, too concerned about my job and the plans I had, too afraid to raise my voice and demand something be done.

So, what I didn't want to have happen, the thing I had feared would happen, began to happen...

I could see my child starting to slip through the cracks of a system that didn't understand him or the help he needed. They saw him only as a disruptive, undisciplined, unfocused child – deserving of less attention and not needing more.

Determined to keep that from happening, but still without upsetting the apple cart, I used the resources and skills at my disposal as a qualified, full-time high school teacher. We started putting strategies and techniques in place at home to help him. While I knew he needed more, at that time, I couldn't see a way forward to make my voice heard. Every day, we tried different things at home, sometimes learning painfully, through trial and error, what worked for him specifically and what didn't. We continued adding new strategies and techniques, including special tools to use at home. But only at home, because no matter how many years went by, no matter how many helpless, quiet meetings we held with his educational providers, highlighting the differences so clearly evident to us, each and every time, our concerns were dismissed.

So, we struggled on, on our own. It became a constant balancing act for us and our once happy, smiling, laughing child. Time went on, years passed, and in the way of families like ours, while we were happy, we also became more isolated, more lonely, more marginalised, and more inwardly focused. We struggled with working things out on our own, doing things by ourselves, and being continuously ignored or misunderstood.

The pattern of dismissal continued every time our concerns were raised. Whenever this happened, I felt it in the depths of my being. A part of me - I didn't realise it was a growing part of me - felt that I should say something, make a noise, become a nuisance, so they would start to pay attention, but I was always worried - worried about the repercussions on my child if I did, worried about what it would mean for him and for me. My fears had a firm grip on me then, and I couldn't see much past the 'reassuringly 'safe place they showed me.

Instead, days, weeks, months, and years were spent searching and often not finding the answers we sought. We were lost in the generalised, sometimes inaccurate information out there, feeling increasingly alone. All the while, I was frantically juggling to successfully maintain my full-time, highly demanding, highly stressful teaching job. I didn't know I was walking towards the perfect storm brewing ahead of me.

That perfect storm came with the birth of my second child.

The years of juggling, struggling, balancing, bottling things up, and making futile efforts to change things for my child in a meaningful way came to a head when stress and teacher burnout met postnatal depression head-on.

That's when everything changed! I was forced to stop and look around, to really SEE my world and my role in it. Suddenly, everything looked different. I was looking at the world from a whole new perspective, and I didn't like what I saw.

As I watched my child cradle his baby brother on his lap, I was struck by the realisation that while I had been doing my best for my other 'kids'—my students—I, driven by my fear of taking a stand, had mistakenly expected others to do their best for my child, which they weren't.

With that realisation came a moment of clarity. If I wanted someone to do their best for my boys, it was going to have to be me, and I couldn't do it on a part-time basis.

In the depths of my soul, I knew what that meant, but I fought against it. I still wasn't quite ready to step out of my fear and embrace the courage inside of me. I had all the reasons why nothing should change and constantly argued them with myself. Surely, I didn't have to be that dramatic? After all, I had a well-paying, successful teaching job with good prospects for progression and better pay. That would benefit my children, wouldn't it? Imagine all the things I could put in place for them with that extra money—the help I could afford to pay for. Besides, doing without my salary would have a massive impact on our family. How could that be good for us?

No matter what arguments I put forward, one truth remained: if I wanted something different for my children, I would have to make a different choice.

Knowing the time was now, my hands shaking, filled with uncertainty at what the future would bring and what my decision would mean for us, feeling fear in every fibre of my being but still determined to do it, I took a deep breath, summoned my courage, typed up my resignation letter, and emailed it to the HR department. I wouldn't be returning after maternity leave. It was done, and my life has never been the same.

In the years that followed, we have faced emotional, mental, physical, and financial hardships and difficulties. We've known what it is to be homeless and hungry, but with courage and the grace of God, we've moved past it. Life continues to have its share of challenges. It would be unrealistic to expect otherwise. It is the nature of life in general and definitely the nature of living with, and parenting, autistics.

Even so, having the courage to take that decision to prioritise my family shifted the course of everything. It was as though a veil had parted, and I had clear sight. It has made a world of difference to me, my children, my family, the steps I took and keep taking moving forward, the passion I found within myself, my vision for the future, my roles in life, and the business I'm building today—helping young adult autistics.

Following that decision, with the newfound time and determination I had, and armed with my years as an experienced teacher who had worked with a wide and varied range of students, I could now build up a list of the differences I noticed in my child, with the tools, techniques, and strategies we had at home compared to the absence of them at school. Finally, after almost a decade of asking and being ignored, I had the evidence I needed for my eldest child to start a formal assessment of his developmental and educational differences.

The assessment process took time, but eventually, just before he turned 17, my oldest was formally diagnosed with high-functioning autism. It was only possible because I was now present every day, determined to make sure he didn't fall through the cracks again! Now, I was confident enough to ask for and be given the allowances, help, and accommodations he needed. He could finally have the same tools and strategies in an educational setting, which complemented those he had at home, to give him the opportunity to rise above other people's misconceptions and the flawed expectations that had followed him since the age of 4.

Having realised there is strength in feeling fear, acknowledging it, and taking action anyway, I could now recognise those moments and choose differently. It made a difference when we noticed traits in my younger child that indicated he, too, had developmental differences. Having that formal diagnosis for my eldest child meant that when I raised my concern about my younger child, I was listened to. Between that and being able to offer evidence and examples from all the time spent with him—the result of walking away from my teaching career to focus on my family.

The road to assessment and diagnosis for my younger child was so completely different. Regardless of the opinion of others, the choice was made early on to take his education a different route so he could develop naturally, without the stigma and pressure to conform that his brother had had to endure. My presence, my observations and awareness, my growing willingness and ability to advocate clearly and confidently for my child, my older child's struggles, and his diagnosis—all combined to speed up the process for my younger child. By the time he was five years old, he was assessed as having ASD+. All of this has and continues to shape so much of his acceptance of his world, his life, his approach to himself, and his autism.

In the years since I felt 'that 'fear and stepped forward anyway, my children aren't the only ones who have had the benefit of time and attention. There are times I hardly recognise myself as the person I used to be.

I spent the first few years just focusing on my children and making sure I was doing whatever I had to, to put in place the things they needed. In doing that, I found within myself a depth of being I hadn't known existed, and I began to truly learn about myself, which began my ongoing journey of personal development and growth.

Over time, I realised my own neurodivergence. I recognised my resilience, drive, determination, strengths, skills, abilities, and a desire to make a difference. Through coaching and mentoring, I found a different way to combine my knowledge and experience, teach and educate, and share my vision.

But something was missing.

Knowing how isolating the years had been for us, how lonely and confusing at times, how characterised by fear and dismissal, and how many families, teenagers, and young adult autistics silently struggle every day, I had another choice to make. I could stay safely in the shadows and keep doing what I was doing or continue on the path I'd chosen all those years ago. I could once again take hold of my courage and step forward, out of the shadows into the spotlight, despite my fear, to share my story as a late realised neurodivergent woman parenting autistic children. More than that, I could use my skills, knowledge, and experience to guide the future of so many young adult autistics by helping them find the courage to step out from behind the misconceptions and flawed expectations of others.

Recognising this as another turning point, I reflected on the changes of the last few years.

I finally realised the power of choosing courage over fear as I deliberated on whether I wanted to go back to letting my fears drive me or whether I wanted to look past them, find the other side of the coin again, hold my head high, and move forward on my own terms every day.

After the lessons of my life that have allowed me to see the two faces of courage and fear, the choice is clear. I'm Moon Sade, an Autism Success Mentor who chooses courage over fear and takes one step forward every day.

As you read my story, I want you to know that despite the stories we tell ourselves, if it's possible for me to find courage within myself, then it's possible for you, too.

***

To contact Moon:

Phone Number: +44 7863 715 489

Email: hello@autism-in-disguise.com

Website: www.autism-in-disguise.com

LinkedIn: www.linkedin.com/in/moonsade

Facebook: https://www.facebook.com/moon.sade.754

Vipin Tyagi

My story starts in New Delhi, India where I was born however continues in the US soon after. I moved to New Jersey at 9 months with little to no memory of life before this. Jersey City, NJ provided many beautiful experiences from elementary school up until high school. Being one of the most culturally diverse cities in the country, I was exposed to all kinds of people in a single environment that helped shape much of my worldview. From here, studying Biomedical Engineering in college taught even more lessons but where I really started to explore what life could be was in the years following.

Post college, I think most start to explore different possibilities personally and professionally, and this was my case as well. My love for reading, entrepreneurship, travel, etc. became center points. Upon a move away from home and across the country, becoming comfortable with the uncomfortable provided a plethora of growth moments. Finding and speaking to world class coaches, speakers and all of the above has been truly engaging. The goal still remains to develop skillsets and assets that can serve the world in some positive sense. Meeting people, engaging in the personal development community and finding good people doing good work globally continues to be what brings me joy ultimately.

Following Our Inner Whispers

By Vipin Tyagi

Life has a specific ebb and flow to it I've realized over the years into adulthood. A mixture of circumstances and intuitive pulls lead you to specifically the places you need to be. Often times the same circumstances and intuitive pulls lead you to meeting the specific people you are meant to meet as well. This did not always register or make sense to me however. Life growing up was pretty interesting. I was a very curious kid and growing up, the world and people around me provided plenty of opportunities to quench this thirst.

My parents both immigrated from India, with the usual intentions of most who do the same.. hoping for a better life for themselves and ultimately their children. Jersey City, NJ was home and where I would find myself at just under a year old with my parents and an older sister. My father ran a modest clothing business in Union City, NJ; a Hispanic centered city full of thriving local businesses, summer parades and endless miles of bustling sidewalks to wander as a child looking to understand the world. Long days and even long nights were spent in that clothing store growing up. Memories of my mom helping my dad orchestrate the daily tasks any store owner goes through still sit vividly in my mind, the children would play, the parents would labor to earn a living. As I said earlier, a pursuit known all to well amongst most immigrants arriving to the USA.

As is still the case today, life was full of exploration during childhood. Garnering a sense of what knowledge, communication and experiences was all about became the natural order of life, all very organically. This was still the generation where kids played in the streets after school, raced down sidewalks with bikes and got yelled at by parents because the dinner was getting cold inside the house. There was generally an understood hierarchy of the "cool crew" on the block and we all were just doing our best to make our way in this social ecosystem. Looking back, the social dynamics and challenges of everything from figuring out how to contribute, fit in to this community and also break the mold puts such a smile on my face. As is the case for most times we look back on periods in life, the so called "challenges" that seemed monumental then are things we laugh & smile at now.

Life went through a series of transitions from elementary school into high school. Street dodgeball games turned into afterschool activities while evenings spent at the family clothing store turned into evenings in my bedroom getting lost in the creative corners of my mind through artwork. For many, high school becomes the period of life where you start to comprehend where and how you fit into different circles socially. Community and friendship is a cornerstone of happiness until the end of our lives, and high school becomes a testing ground of both. Luckily for me, finding my crowd was an incredibly seamless and organic phenomenon and for this I am incredibly grateful. From representing my state & school in an internation science fair to exploring my love of writing, academically high school provided enough to spark premature interests to keep my mind occupied.

College and the years following became much more about internal development and honing in on where life was & what it could ultimately become. Studying Biomedical Engineering provided its own academic highs and lows, but when I look back on college, what comes to mind are the learning lessons socially and emotionally. Those years were an incredible exploration of human nature, not just of others but my own as well. The uneasiness and angst of trying to forge some kind of productive path ahead collided with the enjoyment of new friendships and newfound hobbies. In some sense, I emerged into the "real world" post college with an incredible sense of wonder and curiosity as to where this could all go, feeling as if the ride had not even begun yet. Diving headfirst into corporate full-time roles, I had my first intuitive whispers that there was perhaps more to this equation than I thought in the years before.

Once you comprehend the notion of "untapped potential", life really begins to open up in some miraculous ways. The years in my 20's were largely spent exploring what this meant and how this puzzle can or should be approached. From flying to Tony Robbin's seminars to dabbling my feet into entrepreneurship for the first time, the memories were fond & lessons plenty. Concentration on a singular goal is perhaps what many would say is an important key to success however this strategy was never something I adopted too well. My curiosity led me to explore various projects and interests, looking and hoping to find any sense of something that would appeal enough to become "the thing" to ultimately pursue. I know now, both the exploration phase of this but also the commitment to a singular approach is necessary.

The experiences of those first three decades in life collectively informed much of what drew my interests in recent years up until now. Personal development, understanding business strategy, networking with some of the biggest coaches and speakers in the world..this became a natural passion of mine. The curiosity to explore the various modalities carried out by facilitators around the world became a fascinating pursuit. In 2021, I packed a few suitcases and moved to San Diego, California to fulfill what was a long time yearning to experience the west coast. This falls into what I refer to as intuitive whispers, something you don't consciously choose to do but feel rather pulled to do. The move while providing me with the novel experience I was seeking added some unexpected yet welcome surprises in addition. There, completely by chance, I met some folks involved in this very book's making. That happenstance would in effect put me on an entirely different trajectory of where and how I spent my time and curiosity.

I dove into the world of coaches trying to make a difference in the world. Health coaches, leadership coaches, holistic wellness experts, communication consultants, you name it. Learning about their work and the modalities from NLP to PSYCH-K became a fascinating pandora's box to travel into. At the same time, truly understanding human nature and the art of effective listening & communicating became a focal point, not through conscious intention but more from a newly spawned curiosity. Why do some entrepreneurs become successful and others not? How do coaches and speakers translate their work & mission to an international audience hungry for the knowledge? What are the mindset shifts a coach or brand owner needs to make to properly scale a business both for impact and profit?

These are the types of questions I became curious about. Writing this, I can say I do not have all of the answers to these fundamental questions just yet either. Speaking to coaches and speakers around the world, many doing the type of impactful work that would sometimes make my jaw drop, became less "work" and more fun. Little did I know, the topics my younger self was curious about became the same topics I was now given the ability to explore at a much deeper depth.

The time from my schooling and years in corporate back home served as useful experiences that gave me valuable tools and insight as well. Education alone teaches you how to not only consume information, sometimes copious amounts at once, but process and ultimately make something useful out of it. Working for various large organizations teaches everything under the sun from strategic planning to proper handling of disputes. Taking from these two, I slowly started to craft what the application of these skills could look like in my work outside a corporate role. I became curious what a transition for someone looks like when they choose to move away from a path they have become far too familiar with to one less known. Ultimately the biggest alignment and similarity I found is the ever-applicable skills of listening and communicating effectively. This is a common reason many don't forge a solid network. This is the reason many don't properly scale their personal businesses. This is the reason why stagnancy often befalls many both professionally and personally. I myself have fallen victim and in some cases still do, the difference is I am much more aware of it nowadays.

Proper communication and understanding of one's needs especially in a coaching or speaking business allows me to be a better connector to where I can potentially help them find what they are looking for to solve for that need. Working on book projects where some distinguished coaches and speakers share their stories and purposes gives me this platform where I can use these acquired skills to help them expand their own voice. The lessons that come out of authentic curiosity become incredibly applicable when speaking to business owners seeking opportunities or a larger platform I've found. This holds especially true in the personal development space.

Not everything is for everybody, and you have to be willing to approach everyone with an open mind as to whether the solution you have is or is not applicable to them and their work. If it is not, there is always opportunities to direct them to look somewhere where the answer may be. I've gathered a certain appreciation for the art of listening with the intention of providing value rather than listening just to respond. Looking back, these were the same lessons the last few decades were busy teaching me through the various stages of school, work and entrepreneurship.

A large part of what I enjoy spending time in is speaking to personal development professionals and as mentioned, either providing value via book or speaking opportunities to help them expand their reach or connecting them to others in the industry that can help them do the same. Building out my network in this space has become a fun endeavor that has opened my own eyes into the incredible work going on around the world. This is happening across continents by leaders in the space but also those just trying to break in. Speak to a coach who is fresh to the game, with a soul driven mission to impact their audience and it quickly becomes the most engaging conversation of the week. The purpose behind their mission, the awareness of marketplace need, the knowledge that going at it by themselves is often not the best approach. These become noticeable traits of folks that fit this audience. Yet the most fascinating and admirable trait I observe talking to many new coaches or speakers in this space is the sheer conviction they carry that they will be the one to make that needed difference in whatever their field is. I often say there is no lying around this, either you can tell someone really lives and believes they are the change maker, or they do not. Those that do, often become the ones that really move the needle in significant ways whether it's the coach working with victims of trauma or the speaker looking to ignite change in an audience of executives. I've often wondered why some have this strong conviction and others either find it along the entrepreneurship journey or never at all. Part of it may come down to the innate characteristics of the individual but I've observed much of it stems from life's trials and tribulations one had to endure. You go through a very specific experience, work hard to overcome it, then find yourself in a position to help others do the same. I have had beautiful conversations from change makers around the world who see this not as an option but a necessity, something they must do for others going through the same. In a space where there can be a mixed bag of effective and ineffective professionals, this passion and burning conviction for impact may be one of the few qualities that separates those two camps.

Spending much time in this world of change makers looking to make an impact on lives globally, you pick up on the nuances of the trade and the various ways folks approach it. Some find joy in the intimate 1 on 1 interaction with an individual in person or on camera, being fully present with their individual needs and providing customized solutions. The work itself especially when it comes to exploring past trauma can be arduous & long, I've gathered. Yet there are coaches out there that even with opportunities for real audience growth and thus real financial expansion will purposefully choose to stick to their small-scale personal model. Seeing this and understanding the commitment they have to working with a select group of clients for months or in some cases years at a time until genuine healing has occurred, I have come to appreciate this approach for those that choose it. For others, a transition to larger group coaching or retreats becomes the norm. The larger impact at scale this can provide becomes a driving factor. Then there are even others that choose to explore beyond the client-based coaching and dedicate most of their bandwidth to speaking on stages or being hosted on various media. Observing all these approaches and the driving factors behind them has given me an incredible education on the "why" that drives entrepreneurs in this space. Financial success is rarely the dominant driving factor. Impact always is.

Some of the most common words you'll hear speaking to hundreds of coaches, speakers, workshop facilitators, etc. from around the world are "impact", "change", "heal" & "results". In many ways after having so many of these conversations, I've absorbed new meanings to these words myself and that ih and of itself has been a gift. In fact there are many lessons I've learned working on projects in the personal development space for a few years now with some of the prominent names. One that stands out glaringly is that some of the best understand the notion of scaling a business properly while delivering immense value to the audience. Others in many cases are passionate about delivering immense value but do not exactly see it through the lens of them running a business that needs strategy behind it. Observing this from my conversations has been an interesting study for me. There are certainly two camps that co-exist in the same ecosystem, one with hungry coaches with serious entrepreneurial aims and another with hungry coaches who whether intentionally or unintentionally do not aim to achieve certain levels of feats in the business of coaching.

The journey from being curious about how the world operates socially to deepening curiosity at our human nature has led me to some beautiful opportunities. From high school days in an incredibly diverse part of the country to mixing with movers and shakers after college, the lessons on what inspires entrepreneurs especially in this personal development space have been beautiful to learn.

One thing is for sure, you can never learn all that you need to without some tremendous mentors and helping hands come into your life to propel that forward. For this I consider myself very lucky. I always was and continue to be a big proponent of mentorship whether for our personal goals or business-related ones as well. The interactions I've had the privilege of having with those in the industry have not only taught me the lessons mentioned here but many have become good friends and mentors along the way. Every interaction has almost something you can glean insight from I've learned. Sometimes its more about how curious we are to ask the question that sparks that kind of value driven engagement. Asking a coach how their hypnotherapy differs from other modalities or inquiring with a speaker why some audiences are moved by their work and others not. For me, these come not as a way to prolong a conversation but from genuine curiosity, and genuine curiosity I've learned is where a plethora of great knowledge stems from.

The journey to speak, help and connect with more coaches, speakers or just about anyone else in this space continues. The personal development industry is a rapidly growing one and to find those doing solid genuine work is a fun endeavor. More than anything I always emphasize the importance of authentic curiosity and listening to our intuitive whispers. Many things, including the opportunity to dive into the space, have simply flowed from there for me and I am certain this trend won't come to an end anytime soon.

Start with the bottom line!! Book 2 things:

***

To contact Vipin:

changecoauthors@gmail.com

Afterword

Life is always a series of transitions... people, places and things that shape who we are as individuals. Often, you never know that the next catalyst for change is around the corner.

Jim Britt and Jim Lutes have spent decades influencing individuals to blossom into the best version of themselves.

Allow all you have read in this book to create introspection and redirection if required. It's your journey to craft.

The Change is a series. A global movement. Watch for future releases and add them to your collection. If you know of anyone who would like to be considered as a co-author for a future book, have them email our offices at support@jimbritt.com.

The individual and combined works of Jim Britt and Jim Lutes have filled seminar rooms to maximum capacity and created a worldwide demand.

The blessings go both ways as Jim and Jim are always willing students of life. Out of demand for life-changing programs and events, Jim and Jim conduct seminars worldwide.

To Schedule Jim Britt or Jim Lutes as your featured speaker at your next convention or special event, email Jim Britt at: support@jimbritt.com or Jim Lutes at: mindpowerpro@yahoo.com

For more info on Jim & Jim visit: www.LutesInternational.com or www.JimBritt.com

For information on Jim Britt's online coaching course Cracking the Rich Code: http://CrackingTheRichCode.com

Master your moment as they become hours that become days.

Do something remarkable today! Your legacy awaits.

Blessings,

Jim Britt and Jim Lutes

www.ingramcontent.com/pod-product-compliance
Lightning Source LLC
LaVergne TN
LVHW010201070526
838199LV00062B/4443